Professional Learning through Reflective Artmaking

A Pedagogical Portfolio

Wendy M. Caughey Milne

Wisdom of Practice Series

Learning Moments Press
Pittsburgh, PA

Professional Learning through Reflective Artmaking:
A Pedagogical Portfolio
Published by Learning Moments Press
Pittsburgh, PA 15139
Learningmomentspress.com

ISBN-13 978-0-9993638-9-8
BISAC Subject: Education; Arts in Education (EDU057000);
Education: Professional Development (EDU 046000);
Education: Collaborative and Team Teaching (EDU0450000)

Onix audience Code: 06 Professional & Scholarly

Book Layout: Mike Murray, pearhouse.com

About the Cover Background

The background of this book cover is taken from a large, 12-page fold-out portfolio I created to demonstrate my learning in a course on qualitative research. On one side I merged sketches with handwritten passages and colorful graphs to represent my various interests of study. The other side consisted solely of warm-colored tissue paper gradually morphing from four simple rectangles of color into overlapping layers of torn pieces of the paper. When asked which side I created first, I explained that the colors came before the words, because I come to know through visual representations. I could see my professors' "aha" moment as their word-centric assumptions shifted. They gained a new appreciation for the meaning of arts-based educational inquiry, and I gained a focus and process, not only for my dissertation, but for ongoing professional learning.

*I dedicate this book to Maria for
bringing back the artist in me.*

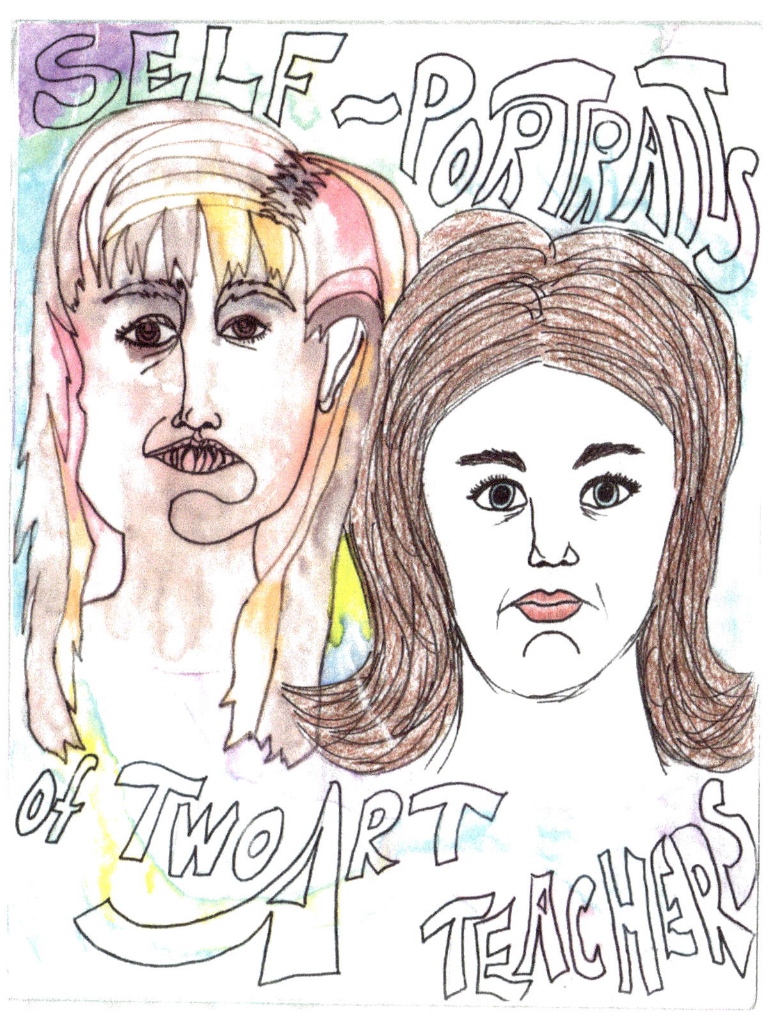

*I would like to express my deepest appreciation
to Heide Wajdic Heddinger for joining me
on this journey. Thank you, Thank you.*

Table of Contents

Foreword

For many years, I have been part of a study group, the members of which share a history of exploring an interpretivist worldview through our individual projects—dissertation writing or other scholarly works for publication. It was at this study group where I met Wendy Milne, and it was at our study group table where I and the others had the good fortune to experience a groundbreaking moment in our thinking: Wendy had *drawn* her way into inquiry and into discoveries about her teaching practice. This inquiry, what she refers to as reflective artmaking, was the focus of her dissertation. I was spellbound. Here was an example of what Elliot Eisner meant when he wrote about what the arts can contribute to education—how different forms of representation can imbue our perceptions with a new kind of clarity, providing fresh perspectives. Art as a meaning-making catalyst was, in all its manifestations, a subject I was particularly interested in, having written about my own teaching in the form of fictive stories, a genre that reflected my belief in the power of story to elicit insights about my teaching. For these reasons, I felt naturally drawn to Wendy's work with the visual arts, but Wendy's dissertation was especially exciting to think about because she was moving to deeper understandings about her teaching practice from her artwork (pictures) to her written words. I was struck by Wendy's courage to forge what seemed to me to be her own brand of powerful reflection and by her collaborative spirit: she had invited her student teacher at the time to embark upon this inquiry with her.

Artist-teacher Wendy Milne's remarkable, award-winning dissertation[1] provides the foundation for this book, in which she shares with her readers her deeply personal learning journey as a teacher. This book is artful, intelligent, courageous, and compelling. It represents

---

1   Milne, Wendy M. Caughey. *Reflective Artmaking: Implications for Art Education,* 2000. UMI ProQuest Digital Dissertation. AAAT9974457

Wendy's continued exploration of her pedagogy at the intersection of art, reflection, and professional learning.

In *Professional Learning through Reflective Artmaking: A Pedagogical Portfolio*, Wendy invites us to witness her experience as a reflective art maker. She uses the metaphor of an art portfolio to organize her journey that begins with her "longing to create art" that would enable her to "engage in a personally meaningful, professionally enriching, and continually renewing process of learning." With each portfolio entry, Wendy makes visible unfolding layers of rich pedagogical insights borne of a desire to understand how she might study her pedagogy through a process of reflective artmaking. Moments from her practice that claim her attention but to which she cannot assign meaning become sites of study. What she cannot initially articulate— she draws, and, from her drawings, she is able to express her feelings, examine the nature of her thinking, and theorize. For Wendy, the act of creating art is both the process and, ultimately, the artifact of her reflecting; and her drawings remain forever relevant and instructive for her. Wendy's quest to "be a better art teacher" is hugely significant. Her use of the word *artmaking* holds important implications for educators: she encourages us to understand artmaking as an aesthetic mode of knowing—a vehicle for reflection.

Wendy's steadfast pursuit to study her teaching practice finds form in her pedagogical portfolio portrayals, which give us an intimate view of her reflective artmaking process as well as her evolving relationship with the concept of reflection. With great vulnerability, Wendy moves from what she describes as a very narrow idea of what it means to reflect to an increasingly more complex understanding—a scholar-practitioner stance of inquiry. Her reflection is fueled by her unflinching commitment to unearth and interrogate her assumptions and unexamined teaching practices and by the brilliant connections she makes with scholarly discourses that help her bring into focus troubling classroom episodes so that she may more clearly see what they represent and how she might learn from them. She tells us that her research challenged her "to reevaluate what I think and do as an art teacher" and compelled her to "understand more deeply the process of teaching art." In analyzing her images and in explicating the concept of reflective artmaking, Wendy's epiphanies are also ours in that, as her readers, we come away from this vicarious experience appreciating more fully the power of aesthetic modes of representation to provide a pathway to inquiry through reflection and to ongoing personalized professional learning.

Wendy's innovative work with reflective artmaking vividly illustrates how continuous occasions for personalized professional learning are embedded in our teaching practice. Teachers who reflect on the complexities of their practice in sustained and meaningful ways are, in essence, designing their own learning experiences and, in the process, enacting their professional agency. When Wendy invites her student teacher Heide to collaborate with her on this reflective artmaking project, she adds another dimension—(What happens when a seasoned educator and a novice teacher co-create a learning experience for themselves?)—not only to her study but also to her stewardship role as Heide's mentor.

Over the years, I have supervised many student teachers and observed many configurations of interaction between preservice teachers and their mentors. I have never seen a collaboration such as Wendy and Heide's. Their commitment to the reflective artmaking process demonstrates their willingness to risk, to become vulnerable with each other as they surrender to a task that, as Wendy tells us, was "simply defined and ambiguous at the outset." Trusting in the process and in each other, the questions they pose to one another along the way—questions about themselves as artists, as teachers, as learners on a reflective artmaking journey—illustrate their capacity for metacognitive reflection, for problematizing their pedagogy in order to study it and to learn how to continue learning throughout their careers. I imagine that Heide will never forget her student teaching experience with Wendy. Their collaboration exemplifies what can be gained when teachers design their own personal professional learning pathways.

When Wendy and Heide decided to facilitate their own professional learning to study their discipline and their pedagogy, they became their own learning network. Today, more and more teachers are enacting their professional agency in just this way. Teachers are increasingly engaging in curriculum development through collaborative partnerships at the school level and beyond, demonstrating innovative leadership in their role as learner-centered curriculum designers—in their work within various contexts and systems and in their own professional learning agendas. As the rapid pace of technology ensures that the context of education will continue to change, with the familiar institutional structures and routines of education shifting, it will be teachers, working together, forging new learning pathways and innovative approaches, who will help us meet the education challenges that we face.

I am grateful that Wendy Milne has shared her reflective artmaking journey with us. The rigor of her inquiry process, her commitment to her professional growth, and the example of mentorship she provides in her authentic collaboration with her student teacher reflect the scholarship and the artistry of her teaching practice.

— Patricia L. McMahon, PhD

Preface

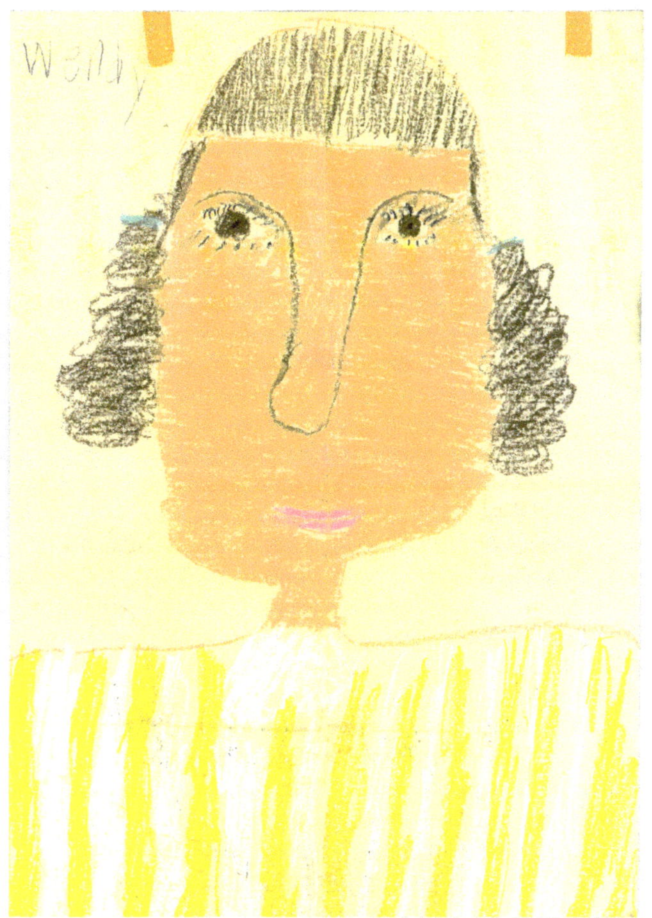

The Call of Art—Early Reflections

My first recollection of art class is from second grade. Decades later, I can still recall the lesson easily, more easily than any other academic lessons I learned in elementary school. During that particular school year, the art teacher taught us how to draw self-portraits. I remember him coming into our classroom and instructing us to fold the paper into quarters so we could draw our face in proportion. I can see myself selecting the exact shade of yellow that was in my favorite dress and drawing spiraling lines for ponytails falling down the sides of my face. When I shared this memory with my mother, she miraculously found the original drawing in her attic. The image represents my desire to work in the field of art, my early interest in portraiture, and my aesthetic way of knowing.

Several years after learning to draw a self-portrait, I was struggling with math and dreading the task of writing our times tables. I devised a system to write out each table, with the goal, not to learn my times tables, but to construct various visual patterns and practice my handwriting.

My best moments in school were spent in art class and when we were permitted to draw at the end of the day. The pleasure of drawing remained throughout my schooling and culminated in my choosing art education as a career.

A Return to Artmaking

Although art has always been an important part of my life, I had little time to devote to artmaking once I began my career as an elementary art teacher. Despite my desire to be the best art teacher I can be, my teaching schedule left little time to think about my pedagogical decisions and actions. The lack of time for reflection resulted in a sense that something was missing in my teaching; a sense that I was not as good as I could be, but not knowing what else I might do. My hope was to work collaboratively with classroom teachers to incorporate art into *their* subject areas. My overtures were met with smiles and requests for holiday decorations and no desire for substantive collaboration. Clearly they saw me as little more than a bulletin board decorator, which engendered frustration, and over the years, anger.

Working alone, I pursued various avenues to continue my professional learning, ultimately enrolling in a doctoral program in art education. Concentrating on my academic studies, I pushed my own artmaking activities further into the background. The university, after all, is a place for reading scholarly literature and writing academic papers. Ironically, I had fallen into the trap of treating artmaking as a "frill" to my doctoral studies—until one evening I was invited to visually represent my reflections on interpretive inquiry. This invitation, coupled with an earlier suggestion that I delve into the literature on teacher-reflection, freed me to resume artmaking as a way to study my pedagogical practice. With a sense of renewed energy, I embarked on a study of my pedagogy through a process of reflective artmaking.

I began my study in the fall of 1998 when I served as a cooperating teacher for Heide, a student-teacher. During her seven week assignment, we engaged in a collaborative process of reflective artmaking. After Heide left my classroom, I continued the process as I completed my doctoral dissertation. Since then, I have continued to reflect on my teaching through reflective artmaking. This book has emerged from this process of on-going professional learning

Reflective Art-Making as Professional Learning

In my early years of practice, I had a very narrow understanding of "reflection." I incorporated reflection into my students' artistic practices by using worksheets which directed students to think and write about their completed artwork and the processes they had used to create it. Years later, reading Linda Beck's dissertation, *Teacher Reflective Practice Documenting Reflection in a Teacher Collaborative Group*,[1] I was reminded of the importance of teachers reflecting on their own practice. Beck contends that we cannot teach what we do not know; therefore teachers must reflect if they want their students to do so.

I had assumed I already was a reflective teacher, because I cared about the ways in which I taught and worked many hours outside of the school day to grade and display student art. I also believed that thinking about ways to change my lessons to make them more exciting and more organized made me a reflective teacher. Little did I know that an extensive body of literature on teaching and school reform called for teachers to engage in reflection as a way of improving their pedagogy.[2]

---

1 Linda Beck, *Teacher Reflective Practice Documenting Reflection in a Teacher Collaborative Group* (Unpublished doctoral dissertation, University of California, 1997).

2 For resources on teacher reflection see: Beck, 1997; Bolin, 1999; Brubacher, Case and Reagan, 1994; Burnard and Hennessy, 2006; Galbraith, 1988; Henry, 1999; Livingston, 1999; Onslow and Gadanidis, 1997; Posner, 1993; Schon, 1987; Thunder-McGuire, 1995; Tremmel, 1993. Full citations in Bibliography.

Reflection, it seemed, might help me to address that underlying feeling that something was missing from my practice.

For educational philosopher John Dewey, reflection was not a simple matter of thinking things over as I had assumed. Rather, reflective practice obliges the reflector to contemplate carefully what has transpired and how this information might be applied in the future.[3] Jeanne Smith elaborates on this point:

> Reflective practice in the educational arena is a process that involves a practitioner's ability to delve beneath the surface, to think about events and one's behavior both inside and outside the classroom or school, to examine one's underlying motives for that behavior, and to decide upon future courses of action.[4]

As I discovered, reflective artmaking was a process that involved exactly this type of careful, thoughtful analysis. I came to realize that by drawing upon my longing to create art, I could engage in a personally meaningful, professionally enriching, and continually renewing process of learning.

Purpose and Organization of the Book

In 2000, when I completed my doctorate in education, peers often asked, "What do you want to do with your degree?" Most thought I would want to become a school administrator; many were surprised when I simply stated, "All I want to do is be a better art teacher." Over the years, I have met other teachers who share this desire to remain in the classroom and advance professionally, not through new positions, but through an ever deepening mastery of their pedagogical craft.[5]

---

3 John Dewey, *How We Think: A Restatement of the Relation of Reflective Thinking to the Educative Process* (Boston: Houghton Mifflin. 1933/1998).

4 Jeanne Smith, *Qualitative Focus Group of Study of Crystalizing and Flow Experience in Educators' Professional Development* (Unpublished doctoral dissertation, Indiana University of Pennsylvania, 1998). 72.

5 During the final years of my doctoral work, I was privileged to join a group of like-minded educators. Their stories of studying their practice are recounted in *The Authority to Imagine: The Struggle toward Representation in Dissertation Writing* edited by Noreen B. Garman and Maria Piantanida. Their experiences of participating in a supportive learning community are recounted in *An Invitation to Study Group: A Collection of Think Pieces* edited by Cynthia A. Tananis. Full citations in Bibliography.

Thus, my aim in sharing my reflective artmaking experience is twofold. First, I want to encourage other art teachers to draw upon their aesthetic modes of knowing to study their teaching practice. Second, in a world where art is all too often seen as an educational "frill," I want to demonstrate the powerful understandings that can be generated through aesthetic modes of knowing.

I use the metaphor of an art portfolio to organize the contents of *Professional Learning through Reflective Artmaking*. Each chapter focuses on a *Portfolio Artifact*. Many *Artifacts* were crafted as part of my dissertation inquiry. Others came in the years following completion of my doctorate. Most recently, I have been creating pedagogical portfolios to fulfill the Pennsylvania Department of Education's requirement for differentiated supervision.[6] In addition to the primary image for each *Portfolio Artifact*, I have included images in some chapters to illustrate a more specific point.

Typically, my need to draw is catalyzed by an aspect of classroom life that calls for attention. I consider this a process (not best works) portfolio, because each piece depicts an understanding that continues to evolve as I proceed on my professional journey. Taken together, however, the contents of my pedagogical portfolio portray the teacher I am and the teacher I am always striving to be.

I have organized the *Portfolio Artifacts* around eight broad themes. Although issues embedded in the themes weave throughout many of the individual pieces, each cluster represents a focus of my reflections. I conclude each section with *Reflective Highlights* where I call attention to interconnections among the individual *Portfolio Artifacts* and among *Portfolio Themes*.

The first *Portfolio Theme—The Meaning of Reflective Artmaking* includes two artifacts. The first provides background information about the collaborative process through which Heide and I began to capture our impressions. Early on, I naively thought these preliminary impressions constituted reflective artmaking. Over time, however, I

---

6   Each Pennsylvania school district is given leeway to determine how this requirement can be fulfilled. As a member of my district's planning team, I was able to advocate successfully for the inclusion of visual evidence of my professional learning as specified by the Pennsylvania Department of Education, Educator Effectiveness System—Differentiated Supervision. September 2013.

came to understand that the real work of reflection lay in examining what these impressions meant to me as a teacher. Gradually, a form began to emerge for shaping each *Portfolio Artifact*.

Each piece begins with an image I have sketched to capture an elusive or confusing thought or feeling. I then offer multiple forms of reflection about the image. Drawing from the work of curricularists Maria Piantanida and Noreen Garman, I characterize these forms of reflection as recollective, introspective, and conceptual.[7] Typically recollective reflections provide background on the events that prompted me to create a sketch. Introspective reflections capture my thoughts and feelings about those events and the conceptual reflections convey the meanings of the images in relation to my pedagogy. I elaborate on these forms of reflection in *Portfolio Artifact 3—On the Nature of Reflective Artmaking*.

From this background, I move to the second *Portfolio Theme— Balancing Pedagogical Control and Creative Freedom*. The artifacts in this theme depict the tensions between maintaining order and allowing enough freedom for students to explore and experiment. Threaded throughout these artifacts are my struggles to gain deeper insights into the differences among an art-centered, teacher-centered, and child-centered pedagogy.

Portfolio Theme—Reclaiming Artmaking—Lessons in Empathy includes artifacts in which I question my own abilities as an artist and the quality of the art I am creating. The vulnerabilities associated with making my personal sketches public interplay with the on-going issue of my need for control and the borders between control in the service of my own needs and a structure that allows for student creativity.

The artifacts in *Portfolio Theme—A Posture of Listening* represent my focus on the nature of my relationships with students. Uncomfortable with some of the revelations about my attitudes and beliefs, I struggle toward a more accepting mindset.

As an only child, I am quite comfortable working alone. The artifacts in *Portfolio Theme—Learning through Collaborative Artmaking* depict my growing appreciation for the power of collaboration—among my students and between Heide and me.

---

7   Maria Piantanida and Noreen B. Garman, *The Qualitative Dissertation: A Guide for Students and Faculty*, 2nd ed. (Thousand Oaks, CA: Corwin, 2009).

It is hard to believe more than 20 years have elapsed since I completed my dissertation. During that time, I have continued to reflect on my pedagogical practice through sketching, writing, conversation, and deliberation. In the final three *Portfolio Themes*, I offer several concluding observations as I look back on the process, briefly describe a time of transition following completion of my dissertation, and muse about the future.

ON THE NATURE OF
REFLECTIVE ARTMAKING

A Quest for Aesthetic Order

This theme provides an overview of how I approached the process of reflective artmaking—initially in collaboration with my student-teacher and later on my own. I depict the multi-faceted, intertwining facets of the process and present a rationale for the importance of aesthetic knowing. The *Portfolio Artifacts* in this section may be of particular interest to those who want to gain deeper insight into the process and nature of reflective artmaking, either for their own professional learning or for encouraging art education students to develop this habit of mind.[1]

---

1   See also Milne, 2018.

PORTFOLIO ARTIFACT #2

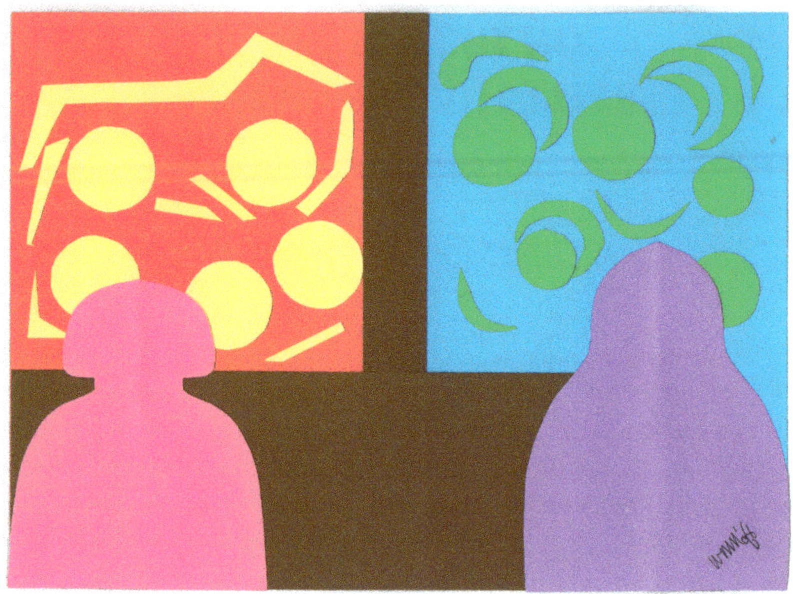

In the Beginning—Initiating Reflective Artmaking

In the fall of 1998, during my ninth year of teaching art at the elementary level, I served as a cooperating teacher during the first seven weeks of the school year. Heide joined me in teaching approximately 750 elementary students at a large rural/suburban school district in southwestern Pennsylvania. Juggling my teaching schedule, my dissertation research, traveling between two buildings and my cooperating teacher responsibilities created a pressure to use my time as wisely and productively as possible. This led me to incorporate my ideas for reflective artmaking into my work with Heide; an idea bolstered by Enid Zimmerman's call for cooperating teachers to "become collaborators who encouraged and allowed pre-service art teachers to be reflective and critical of their own teaching."[2]

---

2   Enid Zimmerman, "Current Research and Practice about Pre-service Visual Art Specialist Teacher Education," *Studies in Art Education* 35, no. 2 (1994): 86.

Additionally, Barbara Caldwell states "In art education we can illustrate and illuminate our teaching by sharing relevant glimpses into our own lives with our students.[3] As we are responsibly open with our students about struggles and strengths, their creative work grows through self-reflection." Further support for a collaborative artmaking process came from the *Student Teaching Handbook* prepared by Heide's university which specifies that, "Throughout the student teaching experience, you are expected to keep a weekly reflection journal."[4]

During our first meeting, as I reviewed the practical details of Heide's student teaching assignment, I wondered when I should introduce the idea of keeping a sketchbook for reflective purposes. What if she did not want to do it? What if it took too much time away from her student teaching? Pushing these thoughts aside, I hesitantly introduced the idea, saying, "Heide, I'm hoping you might be willing to join me in an additional project during your seven weeks of student teaching. I've been reading a lot about teachers' reflecting on their pedagogy, and I've wondered if it would be easier for art teachers to reflect through artmaking." When Heide agreed to my proposal, I suggested she simply draw things about her teaching each day using whatever medium she preferred. I did not tell her how long she should take to create these images or specifically what aspects of her teaching she should be thinking about. I ended by describing a log each of us would keep and the need for weekly videotaped conferences. As the meeting ended, I apologized for the vagueness and brevity of the explanation and admitted I did not have a clearer idea of how we would proceed. "I guess we'll figure it out together," I said as we walked out of the building. (Our confusion about how this might look is depicted in Artifact #2.)

What emerged was a multi-faceted process. Each of us kept an 8 ½ x 11 inch, hard-bound sketchbook to capture visual and verbal texts of our reflections. If we felt constrained by the size of the pages, we drew on separate larger paper or worked on both sides of the sketchbook for larger images or for sequential, cartoon-like drawings. Simple doodles and sketches of daily events were created on some days, while at other

3 Barbara Caldwell, "An Enduring Coterie of Soul Friends: Photographs of Authentic Teaching," In *Women Art Educators V: Conversations Across Time*, eds. Kit Grauer, Rita L. Irwin and Enid Zimmerman, 228-236. Reston, VA: NAEA National Art Education Association. 2003.

4 Seton Hill University, *Student Teacher Handbook* (no date), 5.

times the images were embellished. Many pieces were abstract creations encoding symbolic or metaphoric meaning; far fewer were realistic. Although one of our goals was to examine our pedagogical practices and beliefs, we also created entries about the process of reflective artmaking. In addition, Heide reflected on issues related to student teaching, such as being observed by her advisor and changing grade levels and schools midway through her student teaching placement.

We used a variety of media to express ourselves, but drawing utensils such as crayons, colored pencils, and markers predominated. During the seven weeks, I created one three-dimensional, abstract sculpture. Heide enjoyed using the same colors and materials the students were using in their lessons. Our purpose in using a particular medium was, as Stephen Dobbs suggests, a way "to express teaching experiences, to communicate ideas we learned from teaching, and to explore the unknown aspects of our pedagogy.[5]

In addition to explicating the concept of reflective artmaking, I was curious to discover what would happen when time was allocated for the process. So both Heide and I kept a log that included:

> WHEN: The date and time of reflective artmaking.

> WHERE: Descriptions of our location when we created the reflective art.

> WHAT TYPE OF REFLECTION: Descriptions of how we reflected and the medium used (e.g., drew, printed, painted, verbal description only).

> TIME: The length of time to create the reflective artmaking entries.

> WHAT TRIGGERED THE REFLECTION: A brief sentence or two of what occurred to inspire us to write a reflection.

> FEELINGS AS WE REFLECTED: Description of feelings evoked during the actual reflective artmaking process (e.g., frustration, rushed, stuck for an idea, immersed).

---

5   Stephen M. Dobbs. *Learning in and through Art* (CA: The Getty Education Institute for the Arts, 1998.)

On average a reflective artmaking entry took approximately 30 minutes to complete. Heide's most productive time and place were after dinner in her bedroom. Most of my ideas came while I was driving or showering, so I struggled to capture them on paper before they faded. Having Heide in the classroom provided me with extra time to draw as she was teaching, a point made by Jacqueline Anglin:

> …although having a student teacher can be time consuming it can free the teacher to reflect upon school-related issues as the student teacher takes over responsibilities of the classroom."[6]

Soon after Heide and I started our reflective artmaking process, I added a journal to my sketchbook. I did not share these notes with Heide, and I continued the journaling process after her student teaching experience ended.

Once every five days, Heide and I had a 30 minute conference which we videotaped so that we could record the artwork we were examining. During these conferences, we discussed our sketchbooks, the meanings behind our work, and what triggered the reflective artmaking. Initially, we shared our work sequentially. Later we moved back and forth from piece to piece, frequently returning to previous works to make comparisons. At times, the artmaking process was a focus of discussion as we exchanged information about the techniques or the supplies we used. Our pedagogical practices, however, remained the focus of our deliberations.

On the last evening of Heide's seven-week student teaching experience, we created a collaborative piece of artwork. During the previous weeks, we had brainstormed ideas, finally deciding to depict initial insights gained from the process of reflective artmaking. After three hours of drawing, pasting, and cutting, we created a brightly colored, fold-out collage with written comments incorporated throughout the composition (Image 4: Collaborative Artwork with Heide).

Leaving reflective artmaking simply defined and ambiguous at the outset allowed both of us to explore reflective artmaking as it best

---

6   Jacqueline M. Anglin, "Developing a Creative Relationship with Your Art Student Teacher," *Art Education* 44, no. 2 (1991): 50.

suited each of our needs and to discover what it meant to us. Looking back on the ambiguity with which we entered into a process of mutual reflection strikes me as congruent with the purpose of student teaching described in the *Seton Hill Student Teaching Handbook*:

> Student teaching is one of the most significant aspects of teacher education. In addition to providing preservice teachers with the chance to demonstrate the knowledge, skills, and dispositions they acquired over years of study, this experience also encourages them to explore, experiment, and refine their identities as professional educators.[7]

Following Heide's departure, I began to work with the materials generated during our seven week collaboration to see what meanings they held for me. Over time, I added to this original cache of artifacts. As mentioned above, I entered into reflective artmaking with no clear understanding of what that might entail. By the time I completed my dissertation, I had conceptualized the image that I present in *Portfolio Artifact #3: Layers of Reflective Artmaking*.[8]

---

7   Seton Hill University, 1.

8   For a more detailed account of the relationship between Heide and me see Wendy M. Milne, "The Use of Reflective Artmaking in Pre-service Education," *Mentoring and Tutoring* 12, no. 1 (2004): 37-52.

PORTFOLIO ARTIFACT #3
LAYERS OF REFLECTIVE ARTMAKING

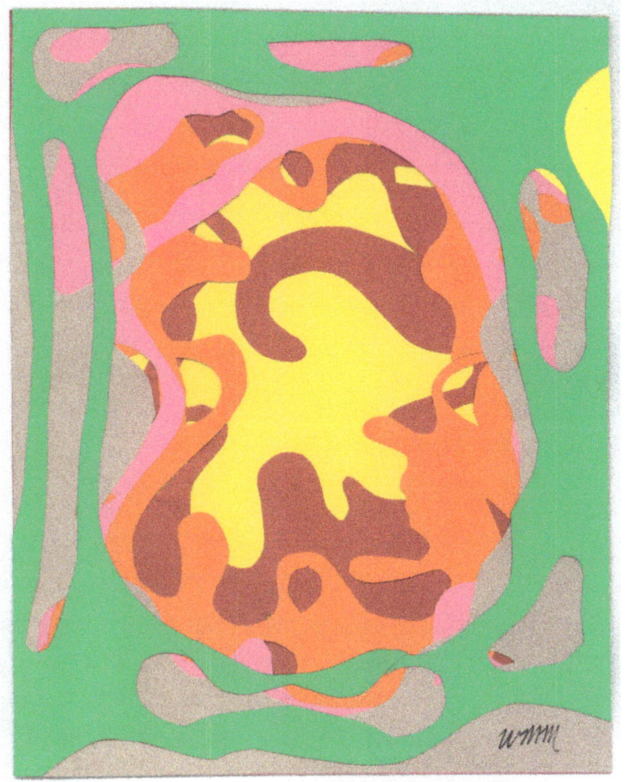

Original Layers of Meaning

In viewing this image, I call attention to two inseparable meanings embedded in the swirling layers of color. These meanings relate both to the multiple, intertwining forms of reflective artmaking and my growth as an artist/teacher/scholar.

Put simply, "reflective artmaking" is a multi-layered, complex, non-linear process of reflecting upon my teaching practice by making art. As Cohen and Gainer[1] and Elliot Eisner point out, artmaking is essentially a quest for order. By giving the world an aesthetic order we "make that world hang together, fit, feel right, put things in balance, and create harmony."[2] Reflective artmaking brings an aesthetic sense of order to the pedagogical event(s) being examined, thus allowing the visually-inclined reflector to more easily communicate to self and others the thinking, insights, and perspectives surrounding teaching practice.

For me, aesthetic order is created through sketching and drawing about a day of teaching—not as a professional artist creating masterpieces—but as a committed art teacher. Capturing my swirling inner dialogue in a sketch enables me to examine past teaching events more closely and/or express underlying feelings that could not be expressed as I taught. The selective process of eliminating or including images in various media and elements of design brings an aesthetic order to my thoughts that might otherwise remain elusive. Elliot Eisner expresses this mode of learning as follows:

> What, then, have I learned from the arts that has influenced the way I think about education? I have learned that knowledge cannot be reduced to what can be said. I have learned that the process of working on a problem yields its own intrinsically valuable rewards and that these rewards are as important as the outcomes. I have learned that goals are not stable targets at which you aim, but directions towards which you travel. I have learned that no part of a composition, whether in a painting or in a school, is independent of the whole in which it participates. I have learned that scientific modes of knowledge are not the only ones that inform and develop human cognition. I have learned that, as constructive activity, science as well as the fine arts

---

1   Elaine P. Cohen, and Ruth S. Gainer. *Art, Another Language for Learning.* (New York: Schocken Books, 1971).

2   Elliot W. Eisner, "Aesthetic Modes of Knowing," in *Learning and Teaching the Ways of Knowing: Eighty-fourth Yearbook of the National Society for the Study of Education*, ed. Elliot W. Eisner (Chicago: University of Chicago Press, 1985), 29.

are artistically created structures. I have learned these lessons and more.[3]

Wanda May, a former public school teacher and artist, relates her experiences of "lingering" in the arts as a way to know her pedagogy. She describes the value of lingering as "making room for herself and reflecting upon her relation to the world and what it means to be in it."[4] Through encounters stretching back to elementary school, May has been able to articulate her beliefs that:

1. Schools need to encourage creative invention and reflection;

2. Teachers must acknowledge usual events in the everyday life of schools, and

3. Questions are more important and provocative than answers.[5]

Both Eisner and May claim that the time spent in the arts improved their understanding of pedagogy. Their views challenge me to reevaluate what I think and do as an art teacher and fuel my desire to understand more deeply the process of teaching art.

As Reid points out, an artist often does not fully know, "except dimly and schematically perhaps, what he is going to create before he creates. He comes to know in the occurrent act of creating."[6] This was certainly the case for me when I visualized swirling, colorful, intricate designs and decided to bring them to life after a particularly long day of teaching. Cutting shapes from colored paper, I wasn't sure what form the image would take. I knew only that I wanted to create a visual metaphor depicting my growth as an artist/teacher/researcher.

Placing the cut pieces over one another seemed to be a good way to represent my realization that reflective artmaking has many forms;

---

3   Elliott W. Eisner, *The Enlightened Eye: Qualitative Inquiry and the Enhancement of Educational Practice* (New York: MacMillan, 1991), 47.

4   Wanda T. May, "The Arts and Curriculum as Lingering," In *Reflections from the Heart of Educational Inquiry*, eds. George Willis and William Schubert (Albany: State University of New York Press, 1991), 140.

5   Wanda T. May, "Teachers, Teaching and the Workplace: Omissions in Curriculum Reform," *Studies in Art Education* 30, no. 3 (1989): 142-149.

6   Louis A. Reid, "Aesthetic Knowledge in the Art," in *The Arts: A Way of Knowing*, ed. Malcolm Ross (New York: Pergamon Press, 1983), 38.

it is not only drawing in a sketchbook every day. The green layer in the background depicts me in the beginning phase of my dissertation, when I naively believed this would be a simple endeavor completed in seven short weeks. As the viewer's eye moves toward the center of the sketch, a gray and then pink layer are glimpsed. The center seems to explode with hot orange, red, and yellow, indicating my passion for reflecting through artmaking, because the process has made me more aware of who I am as a teacher/artist/researcher. I now have what Elliot Eisner calls "an enlightened eye." After viewing the sketch collage, I commented:

> *Before I began to reflect, I was a green color; oblivious to my action (and reactions). As I started to reflect, events and relationships became clearer and brighter. There still exists in me each of these layers. Reflecting did not change me from green to yellow. It helped me to see many more sides of myself, some that I did not like and others that I could strive to be.*

Several months after creating the collage, I realized the colored layers represented not only my own growth, but various forms of reflective artmaking.

Layer 1: Yellow. This layer symbolizes an initial form of recollective reflection—i.e., drawing in the sketchbook. Through drawing I recognized my need to bring an aesthetic order to my life. Daily, I thought about my teaching, but those swirling thoughts were so elusive that I was unable to focus on one thought long enough to come to any sort of understanding. The challenge and excitement of making art about some aspect of my teaching provided the impetus to make time for more focused reflection.

Layer 2: Red. Viewing the sketches and writing about them were another, more introspective, form of reflective artmaking, represented in the second layer. Sitting back to view my sketches allowed me to pause, to think, to reflect. I asked silently, "What triggered this desire to make the image and how do I feel about it now that it is complete?" With these questions in mind, I would write several paragraphs, sometimes pages. Without the images, I struggled to write coherent thoughts and did not enjoy the process. My notes in my written journal took on a mostly documentary format such as "Today I did this…" whereas my written passages in the sketchbook had a more colorful, feeling tone, and many more interpretations were included.

Layer 3: Orange. This layer stands for the dialogue between Heide (my student teacher) and me. Those exchanges helped us further interpret the works of art and the meanings reflective artmaking had for us. Inspecting each other's' art products and discussing the process with a trusted peer allowed me to hear other viewpoints that I had not or did not wish to acknowledge. Heide was also able to gain insights into an experienced teacher's concerns about her own pedagogy.

Layer 4: Pink. This layer represents the process of entering into the conceptual reflection phase as I searched for patterns in the artifacts. This form of reflection was thorny and much more time consuming than the previous forms. I was challenged by the complexity of finding important educational issues within the artifacts and making connections with related discourses. This was one of the most difficult, yet exciting, forms of reflection. Difficult because, as I began, I was not sure in which direction I was headed; often having to retrace my steps. Exciting, partly because of the unknown, but also because this was the first time I read over the artifacts and was amazed with the ideas Heide and I had generated.

Layer 5: Gray. Another challenging aspect of reflective artmaking was the creation of the *Portfolio Artifacts*, depicted in this fifth layer. I assumed that once I selected all the patterns which had educational significance that the remaining phases of my study would be easy. This was not the case. Although the creation of the *Portfolio Artifacts* ran fairly smoothly, decisions of how to organize and present them were difficult.

Layer 6: Green. Finally, the green layer symbolizes the critiques. Engaging in the critique required me to become well-versed in art education theories and practices. This process helped me, not only to understand the significance of the inquiry, but also to begin altering my teaching practice. Without this level of conceptualization the *Portfolio Artifacts* might have been solipsistic and self-serving.

Reflective Highlights on Portfolio Theme Immersion in Reflective Artmaking

Each layer shines through, never completely hidden from view. Although each could stand on its own, the final textural image suggests deeper understandings are reached as I involve myself in each layer. Seen in this light, the collage could be misinterpreted as depicting reflective artmaking as a sequential process. However, the colored layers in the collage symbolize forms of reflective artmaking, not procedural steps. This is why organic, flowing shapes—not rigid, linear ones—are found.

The concept and processes of reflective artmaking need not be followed in any order. Heide, for example, sometimes chose to write in her sketchbook before she drew. At times, we both wrote and drew concurrently. In other instances, our conference discussions inspired me to return to the sketchbook to rework an image or to create a new one. Furthermore, when we collaborated to make a final piece of art, we engaged in many forms of reflective artmaking: (1) we entered into long discussions about teaching, reflection, and artmaking while we created; (2) we drew new images to be used in the collage; (3) we reflected on prior images through discussion and writing to determine which images would best communicate our ideas regarding reflective artmaking, and (4) we added written comments to the collage. I would describe this collaborative process as our early attempts at conceptual reflection.

I also highlighted the small sections in which viewers can see down through the layers. In some cases, when viewing the green section, a glimmer of pink or yellow may shine through, reminders of the back and forth movement of the reflective artmaking process. The layers of reflective artmaking are inextricably intertwined and cannot be divided into steps or stages, such as reflect first and then make art. Inherent in making art is the act of reflection. By anchoring my reflections in artmaking, I am able to weave my swirling thoughts into a coherent message which I am then able to share visually and verbally.

Portfolio Theme

*Balancing Pedagogical Control
and Creative Freedom*

In *Teaching and Its Predicaments*, educator David Cohen describes three terrains of teaching:

> One is the knowledge that teachers extend to learners, and how they extend it. The second is the organization of instructional discourse. The third is teachers' acquaintance with students' knowledge.

As I progressed through the study of my practice, I began to realize that my formal education had focused a great deal on the knowledge associated with the first terrain. My degree and my years of experience had allowed me to develop expertise in the second terrain of instructional delivery. What I hadn't realized until immersing myself in reflective artmaking was the need to cultivate the sensibilities needed to navigate the complexities of the third terrain. Skill in discerning students' knowledge begins with careful attention—watching, listening, and talking with, not at, students. Such attentiveness requires that teachers:

> …step a bit outside their own thought worlds, learn how to explore students' knowledge and ideas from other perspectives, and seek ways to connect students' ideas with the material under consideration.[1]

As will become evident as I present and discuss the *Portfolio Artifacts* under this theme, reflective artmaking allowed me to "step a bit outside" myself. Sometimes what I saw was quite startling, causing

---

1   David K. Cohen, *Teaching and Its Predicaments* (Cambridge, MA: Harvard University Press, 2011), 34, 39.

me to think more carefully about how I was relating to students. Yet simply realizing that I wanted to change my way of relating was not enough. It required conscious effort and practice—an on-going process of learning about myself and what matters to me as I teach. The issues I introduce in this *Portfolio Theme* recur in later themes as well, but in this section I focus on the tensions between my need for control and my desire to promote creativity.

PORTFOLIO ARTIFACT #4

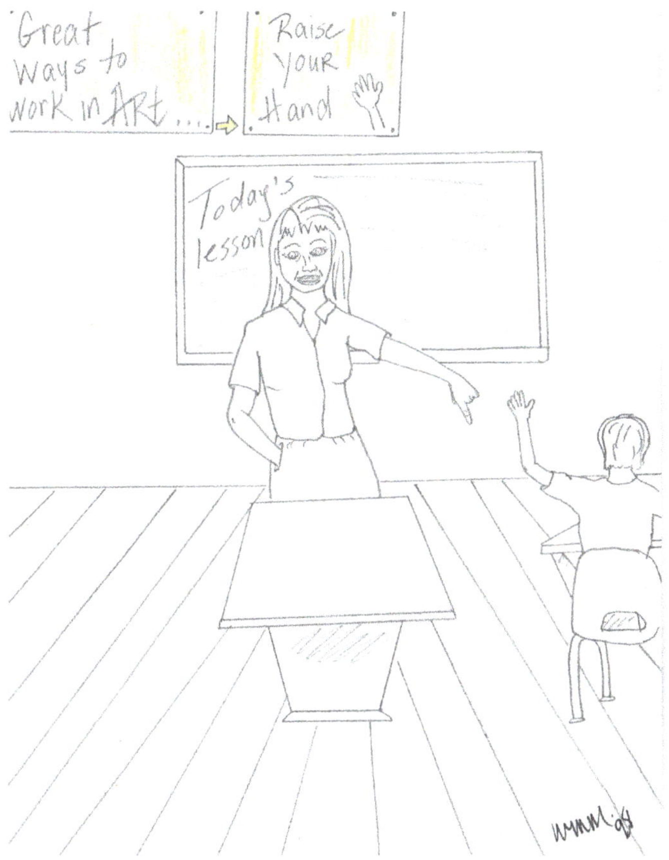

Hands Down

This Portfolio Artifact was inspired by watching a videotape of my teaching a fourth grade lesson on the use of copper foil. I had started by telling the students they would be using the same material from which pennies are made. "Does anyone know what it is?" I asked. "Copper," replied one student. Another student continued to raise her hand, and after a quick look to determine she had no emergency, I gestured for her to lower her hand while I continued to issue instructions. "Right now let's get out your symmetrical mask sketches from last week, and I'll demonstrate how to begin." The students crowded around the table as I sat in the center tracing a drawing onto copper foil. A lively boy named Lucas leaned in to touch the copper, but I pulled it away, explaining that they would get their own piece soon.

Holding up the copper, I imitated their language, "Check this out! Wouldn't it be goofy to do it this way?" Laughter and comments erupted. I described the next step in a strong, clear voice. Robert kept talking so I politely asked him to be quiet. To keep the students focused, I asked again what media we were using and to define the word "symmetrical." I invited the group to tell me if I should add straight or curvy lines around the eyes, and most eagerly responded, "Curvy!" The students then explained the steps, and I complimented them for remembering. While they headed to their seats, I uncovered the chalk board where I had written the steps as a reminder. After encouraging them to start immediately, I strolled through the room, surveying their progress, and commenting, "nice work" or "that's it, keep going."

Several months later, while closely scrutinizing the video, I noted how I used my right index finger to point down when the student continued to raise her hand. Thinking, "I'm not too bad of a teacher," I attempted to draw several images, but none suited my thoughts. The memory of my downward pointing gesture kept returning until I sketched "Hands Down."

In creating the sketch, I began to question the effects of my actions on this particular student and on many others who had been on the receiving end of my pointing finger. Ironically, on the blackboard behind me is a class rule, "Raise your hand if you have a question." What, I wondered, was I really teaching, if I waved down their raised hands, indicating their questions were not important enough to interrupt the flow of the class. Still, I rationalized my actions, remembering the many times I had stopped my instructions only to discover a child wanting to tell me her cat had kittens or she had gone to a fair the previous evening.

I had always been proud of the way I "ran" my classroom. The children seemed to like art. I encountered few discipline problems and derived joy from what I was doing. I was particularly proud that I frequently modified my lessons, not depending on the same tried and true lessons year after year. My supplies were always prepared for the following week's lesson. Even though I held my classes to the 40 minute limit, most students were able to complete their projects, and I was always impressed with their products.

Despite all of this, "Hands Down" called attention to an uneasiness I couldn't quite identify. A journal entry written several weeks later offered the key to interpreting the image.

> *I might be an art teacher for very selfish reasons. I've said it's so great to teach kids, to be around art, etc., but a lot of what I live for is the reward I get from it. I love to hear the kids talking about art or see a wonderful piece of art they've created. I love writing unique lesson plans that make kids say, "Cool, I love art!" I get such a rush when I hear these things—it's like a high for me every time I hear someone say how much they love art class. I think to myself, "I'm the reason. I had something to do with it. These kids know about art and artists, because of me; almost no one else in their lives teaches them about art. I may be their sole influence in the art world and it feels fantastic." Hearing the oohs and aahs after I make a drawing (even if it's pretty pathetic) and hearing them say, "You're so good. Will I ever get that good?" makes me swell with pride. I can't get enough of it.*

> *On the other hand, when the children don't like the lesson, I feel rotten. I take the failures as personally as the successes. It's like going through a drug withdrawal I suppose. When I can't get the drug (praise), it drives me nuts. I'd do anything to get back to the praise. Luckily, in teaching, the "anythings" are usually just revamping the lesson or trying a new medium, or even throwing out a lesson.*

> *But I've taken more serious measures at times. They take the shape of anger when I don't get the praise.*

> *I take my frustration out on the students rather than go back and re-work/re-think the lesson. I blame the students for not understanding what a great lesson I've prepared. I justify it with almost anything, rather than admit I'm wrong.*

My love of art and those "highs" influence my pedagogy—a pedagogy which apparently does not place the children at the center of my thinking. Until I began the reflective artmaking process, I did not realize my lack of focus on the children. Once "Hands Down" focused my attention, I began to wonder what influenced my placing my personal ego needs over the needs of my students.

I attribute my self-centeredness, in part, on the nature of my schedule and my own art education background. Working in two separate buildings, teaching seven grade levels (developmental kindergarten, transitional first grade, and grades 1-5), and over 750 students per week forced me to become efficient and orderly. As Wanda May points out, some art teachers feel such a need to maintain classroom order, they "plan rigid art lessons and routinized tasks in fear of losing control."[1] Having only 40 minutes per class, I feel driven to provide as much art information as possible. Supplementary bus duties and decorating display boards add to my dilemma of finding time to reflect. May could have been writing about me when she says:

> ...teaching provides little time to experiment, to be critically reflective, or to unravel the complexities of one's reality. Because of pressing daily demands, teachers are present-oriented. Teachers most often justify their practice on the basis of feelings, impulse and intuition rather than systematic, critical inquiry because there is little time to be reflective.[2]

My training in undergraduate college did not prepare me to deal effectively with this tight schedule. Instead, my classes were filled with the voices of professors teaching me how to hand-build a clay pot, how

---

1   May, "Teachers, Teaching and the Workplace," 148.
2   May, "Teachers, Teaching and the Workplace," 150.

to apply gesso to a canvas, how to ink a block, or how to utilize the philosophy of Discipline-Based Art Education (DBAE).[3]

Upon graduation, I accepted a teaching position at a district that followed the DBAE philosophy. As a novice working alone without a mentor, I felt inept, and therefore, relied on methods in which I was well versed. In my efforts to cope with an intensive schedule and large numbers of students, I forgot that DBAE could, as Eliot Eisner says, be magical. In my struggle to include the four disciplines in my lessons, I forgot about my students' interests and lives. Reviewing my lesson plans from the first several years, I saw that most of my units focused on different historical periods (e.g., Egyptian or Medieval art) and various artists, techniques, and media. I taught these concepts in a very structured way. I grew to know the children by name, face, and sometimes their siblings. I knew how they behaved and if they were artistically intelligent. Rarely did I talk with them about their homes, their hobbies, their family, or their dreams. Although I frequently changed my lesson plans, rearranged my room, and moved to a different elementary school, I continued teaching in the same general way for eight years, and like many teachers, planned my curriculum before the children arrived each year. When asked, however, I claimed I taught children.

My love of art led me to believe that focusing solely on art was not only appropriate, but beneficial. Everything I did—my organization of the room, my discipline approaches, my unit planning—supported my belief that art was the most important thing in the room. Indeed, noted educator Parker Palmer suggests that a subject-centered environment may be quite successful. By placing the subject, not the teacher or the student, in the center, both rigor and involvement can be had. If either the student or the teacher is placed at the center of the pedagogical circle, narcissism can result. In contrast:

---

3 Briefly stated, DBAE involves designing an overall curriculum and each lesson around four disciplines of art: art production, art history, art criticism, and aesthetics. DBAE was gaining popularity when I was enrolled in college (1984-88), so many of the art educators centered their teaching around this philosophy. For additional information see Aukerman, 1992; Black, 1996; Eisner (Structure and Magic), 1991; Erickson and Katter, 1988; Jeffers, 1990; Kaufman, 1989. Full citations in Bibliography.

> The subject-centered classroom is characterized by the fact that the third thing [the subject] has a presence so real, so vivid, so vocal, that it can hold the teacher and students alike accountable for what they say and do. In such a classroom, there are no inert facts. The great thing is so alive that teacher can turn to student or student to teacher, and either can make a claim on the other in the name of that great thing. Here, teacher and students have a power beyond themselves to contend with—the power of the subject that transcends our self-absorption and refuses to be reduced to our claims about it…
>
> In a subject-centered classroom, the teacher's central task is to give the great thing an independent voice—a capacity to speak its truth quite apart from the teacher's voice in terms that students can hear and understand. When the great thing speaks for itself, teachers and students are more likely to come into a genuine learning community, a community that does not collapse into the egos of students or teacher but knows itself accountable to the subject at the core.[4]

Reading Palmer's argument, I am inclined to defend my ways of teaching and love of art, but I believe that I was not using the subject of art as he suggested. I did place my love of art at the center of my pedagogy, but used it in a way to gain admiration for myself and control my students rather than as a vehicle of communication. The "Hands Down" sketch revealed my tendency to view student "interruptions" as disturbances, as offenses against my love of art. I did not allow the subject to create a learning community. Instead I used it to dictate the behaviors of my students and myself. With this new awareness, I began to examine the benefits of focusing on the children's needs rather than my own. This led, not to a magical, instantaneous pedagogical

---

4   Parker J. Palmer, *The Courage to Teach: Exploring the Inner Landscape of a Teacher's Life.* (San Francisco: Jossey-Bass, 1998), 117-118.

transformation, but rather to a more reflective stance of professional learning.

PORTFOLIO ARTIFACT #5

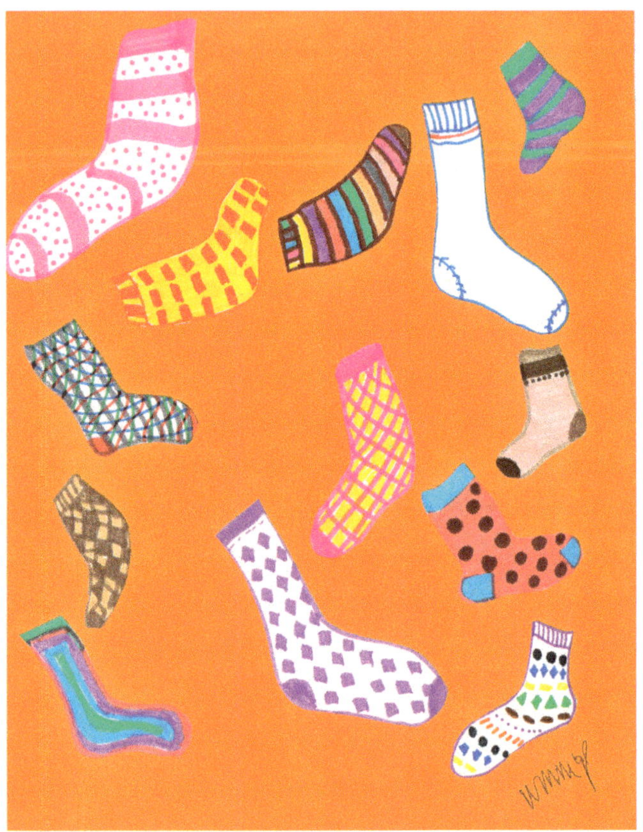

Matching Socks

n the 1997-1998 school year, my district implemented a full-day kindergarten program for students who were struggling. Prior to this innovation, art teachers were never required to teach these youngsters. Now, however, I would be holding weekly 40 minute classes with an age group beyond my teaching experience. I had not been very successful during the first year, so I dreaded the approaching 1998-1999 year, especially since I would now be teaching in front of Heide, my student teacher.

A Discipline-Based Art Education (DBAE) approach had not worked well with this kindergarten group, but I was at a loss as to what to try. I hid my misgivings from Heide by suggesting we jointly develop kindergarten lesson plans. We decided to use a children's books as a starting point. The subject of the book was matching socks, so Heide gathered patterned socks for the children to match. I was amazed to see the children so easily succeeding with this task, even though they were unable to write their names or sit in their seats for more than a few minutes. Watching the children more closely, I saw a group of tired, confused little people.

Later, as they drew sock patterns, one boy took out his scissors and started to cut his paper. I had not planned for any cutting and began to say, "Put the scissors away." But watching him so absorbed in carefully cutting the paper, I stopped myself, realizing he probably needed to practice cutting. "Matching Socks" aided me in seeing the importance of watching and listening to students, something I had not been doing when I took a purely technical approach to DBAE. I sensed a shift in my pedagogy was beginning as I continued my exploration of a "subject-centered classroom.

PORTFOLIO ARTIFACT #6

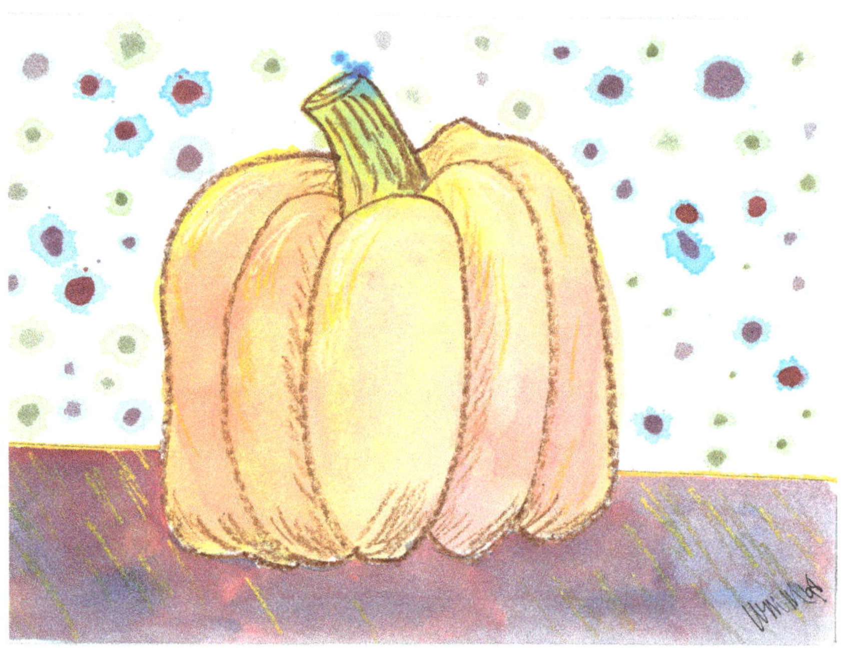

In Control—Out of Control

Despite my determination to shift to a more child-centered pedagogy, my next journal entry reminded me that such change is easier imagined than enacted. I had written about a lesson in which I had dropped blue and yellow food coloring into water to illustrate mixing colors. The children gasped in surprise when green "magically" appeared. Distributing paints for our pumpkin painting project, I decided to let the children experiment on their own. I individually helped the students who were having trouble. So far so good. But I reverted to my step-by-step instructional approach when the children began to add paint to their hand-drawn pumpkin pictures. As the colors bled into one another and the pictures became muddy, I stopped them and demonstrated the correct use of a brush and watercolors. We practiced rinsing brushes and pulling the brush in the same direction over their pumpkin drawing. Like Kathleen Thompson,[1] I often viewed my own success through the students' mastery in their art work, so I did not want them to fail. Later, for my sketchbook entry, I glued down my pumpkin example and wrote, "The children learned to mix colors by hearing, seeing, and doing; they learned to paint correctly."

Further in my writing, however, I wondered if I should have brought in a real pumpkin for them to observe, feel, and smell. I also questioned defaulting to my organized, structured approach when the experimental approach had been working so well in the beginning:

> *The children learned to follow directions, which is something I'm not proud to say as an art teacher. I'm supposed to be enhancing creativity, not direction following. I could say it has to be done, but I wonder if there is another way. Can any class be direction free? I doubt it, but mine could be less directive and more exploratory. I realize this now, but will I change all my lessons? It's so nice to have a variety of prepared, successful lessons that it's hard to imagine writing all new ones. Maybe I can start with Developmental Kindergarten since I have no lessons for them. But who needs more direction than these children? Or do they? Let's see if I can come up with something exploratory for them and see how it works. I might as well explore, too!*

I questioned the organized style of my teaching and asked, "Who benefits more from my controlling the lessons?" Thinking about this the next day, I gave my fifth grade students the freedom to select a project they wished to work on. The children handled the assignment well and appeared to enjoy the independence. That day, I also introduced the concept of a sketchbook, giving each child paper and a folder. I explained that artists often carry a sketchbook with them to record

---

1 Kathleen Thompson, "Teachers as Artists," *Art Education* 29, no. 6 (1986): 47-48.

images and thoughts. For the first time, I showed them my sketchbook, and they appeared to be interested in my work. I felt proud I was able to ask them to do something that I was doing myself.

My need for control, however, had not fully subsided. Although I was starting to realize the students enjoyed the freedom to draw as they chose, I had already copied 25 assignments requiring students to draw specific images which would serve as the basis for grading every nine weeks. Each assignment related, I believed, to student interests—e.g., drawing a futuristic car or drawing a new amusement park. Feeling guilty that I had never checked my assumption about their interests, I encouraged them to use any medium they wished to complete the assignments. Still, this did not fully assuage my guilt. I remembered professors directing me to paint a still life or build a relief sculpture of a city scene. None had much personal relevance, so I completed such projects in a dry, detached manner. Technically they were fine, but there was little of me in the work. Possibly my young students felt the same as they drew image after image to be turned in on a particular date.

PORTFOLIO ARTIFACT #7

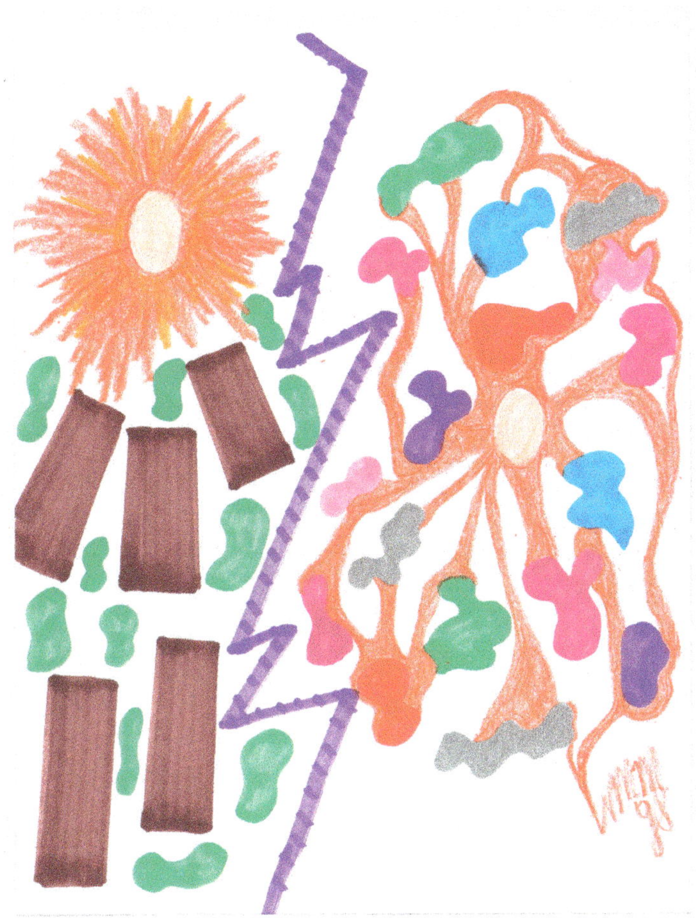

Contrasts

Despite my growing desire to provide students with more freedom, the day after the pumpkin lesson was a disaster. I used a step-by-step lesson that had worked well the previous year, but now as I taught each class, my day got worse. My bad mood, based on personal events at home, compounded the problems. The students were garrulous, failed to follow directions, and had minor arguments. I responded more and more impatiently and gruffly to each of their questions. By the end of the day, in an effort to relieve my stress, I grabbed the oil pastels and scribbled over my sketchbook pages with oranges, yellows, and reds. Into these angry layers I scratched, "Trying to have control makes me feel out of control!"

It seemed my growing desire to be less controlling made the pre-planned lessons less conducive to learning. After calming down and reflecting on my colorfully sketched feelings, I wrote:

> *I had to give so many directions to second grade today. Draw this. Write your name on that. Roll this brayer here. Print there. Switch partners. Roll again. Print again. Clean up. Put the print on the drying rack. On top of this, they were not listening, so I was getting really angry. I'm sure they stopped listening, because I was giving so many directions. At first I thought there was no other way to do this printmaking lesson since they had never printed before. But I suppose I could give them some more responsibility and fewer directions to lessen this problem. Maybe when I try to get so much control, I end up out of control, because the students don't want that. Of course they can't have total freedom, but I could ease up.*

That night I taught at the local college and was struck by the contrast in my teaching of college versus elementary students. My mood shifted almost immediately from frustration to delight. Later that evening, I drew the sketch "Contrasts" about these differences.

The abstract image drawn with markers and crayons depicts me on the left as I am at the elementary school. The students are shown in similar green shapes, indicating my expectation that they behave calmly, quietly, and yet, creatively. "Despite being individuals," I wrote, "I expect all eyes to be on me, the orange shining light surrounding my form." The light reaches out, almost touches some of the children, but never quite reaches them. Those in the back are confined to those seats for the rest of the year, never getting close to the light.

In contrast, the image on the right of the drawing shows how I perceive myself to be as a college instructor. I am placed in the center of the college classroom. I reach out and touch all the students who are different shapes and colors, symbolizing my awareness and encouragement of their individuality. The environment here is sparked with energy, whereas the elementary room is calm and cool. True, my time with the college students was longer; the class size was smaller, and I didn't have to monitor adults for discipline problems. Still, there seemed to be a drastic difference between my two teaching contexts. Driving home, I pondered why I did not attempt to apply my college teaching orientation in my elementary practice.

PORTFOLIO ARTIFACT #8

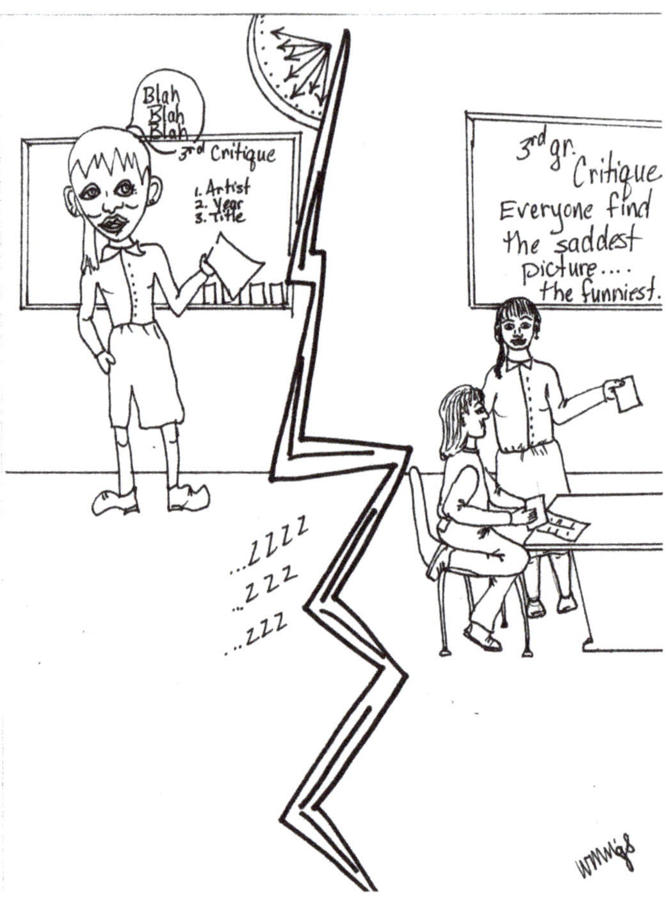

If at first...

As I continued to ponder the different stances I took with college and elementary students, the events of the next day prodded me once again to reflect on my need for control. During a critique lesson with my third grade class, I was frustrated when the students ignored my instructions. This was a well-planned unit in which I selected art reproductions related to the theme "emotions," and asked the children to answer open-ended questions in writing. The questions were based on suggestions in art criticism books, but the students seemed perplexed and weary by the time I finished explaining how to complete the critique. After they left the class, and thinking about my previous night's musings, I decided to change the lesson. Within five minutes I re-planned the critique in a way I imagined would captivate the students and give them more ownership of the activity.

In "If at first...," I am depicted in a cartoonish manner, standing in front of a class, hand on my hip, the clock ticking away as I drone on and on. No children appear in the picture although my large, speaking head indicates there is an audience. To the right, the viewer sees me in better proportion, interacting with the students. On the board are written the words, "Everyone find the saddest picture." No clock is featured, because the time went by pleasantly.

I'm pleased by this Portfolio Artifact because it suggests I'm acting on my reflections to change my pedagogy by becoming more aware of my students' needs. In hindsight, I marvel that early on I believed that "doing" 44 reflections in my sketchbook would completely alter my pedagogical orientation. A year after drawing "Hands Down," I still found it difficult to break the habit of my downward finger gesture. I suppose my reading of the discourses on teacher reflection led me to believe that positive change would happen quickly. However, as Shirley Yokley suggests, "...if there is a change, it may happen in reflection long after the event or encounter...Time is needed to assimilate information and alternative ways of thinking."[1] Well into the process of reflective artmaking, I realized that I had not allowed enough time to assimilate the various layered insights embedded in the artifacts generated during my seven weeks with Heide.

---

1   Shirley H. Yokley, "Embracing a Critical Pedagogy in Art Education," *Art Education* 52, no.5 (1999), 24.

Reflective Highlights:
I Continue to Change

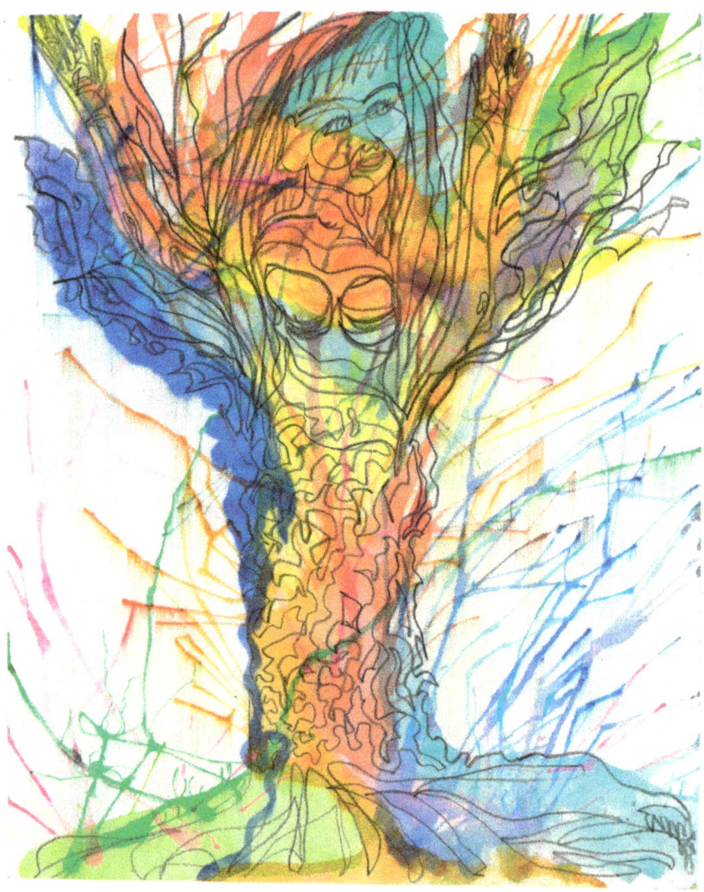

The sketch, "I Continue to Change," depicts my growing realization that becoming a more child-centered teacher would be a slower process than I first imagined. Intricate black, curving lines threaded through watercolors represent my efforts to transform my pedagogical orientation. Adding the visual metaphor of a tree, I transposed the image into bark and limbs reaching towards the sky and wrote:

> *I continue to change after all these years of teaching.
> I could have used the same lessons year after year, but
> I chose not to. I continue writing and teaching new
> lessons. Some are based on my desire to do something
> new or different. Much of the reason I change is due to
> boredom. I like a new challenge as well as something
> exciting for the children.*

Looking back, I see the limitations of thinking that merely changing my lesson plans was synonymous with changing my teaching orientation. When I first interpreted my sketches and writing, I was pleased with the ways I had changed. Ironically, "I Continue to Change," reveals that I had returned—not to the children's needs—but to art and my own needs. Despite my best intentions, my roots remained firmly planted in the soil of my teacher-centered philosophy.

Another irony surfaced as I read the art education literature and came to understand that transforming myself into a child-centered teacher would have been difficult, time-consuming, and perhaps in the end, not entirely appropriate. Further, I realized that I often used teacher-centered and subject-centered interchangeably. This was a false equivalency. My love of art and my educational background influenced a subject-centered, not necessarily teacher-centered, approach: As Elliot Eisner points out:

> …[a] subject-centered approach to curriculum goals, content, and teaching method lays emphasis upon the integrity of the subject matter, its uses in human experience and understanding, and its intrinsic value. In this view of the goals of art education, the teacher is to emphasize the study of art per se; he [sic] is to help the student learn to see and appreciate the work of art not primarily because it will be socially useful for him to do so, but because great products of the human mind and spirit are the proper objects for educational attention.[1]

---

1 Elliot W. Eisner, *Educating Artistic Vision* (Reston, VA: The National Art Education Association, 1997), 59.

I feel that this description applies to me more often than not. Even when I am demanding control in the classroom, which might be construed as teacher-centered, I do so because of my love of art. For example, when students talk out during a demonstration I am less upset about them interrupting me, than I am about them interrupting the art process and art learning. I become angry, because they do not seem to be showing respect towards art.

My "subject-centeredness" also underpinned my practice of keeping student portfolios. I valued all the pieces the children made and viewed them as a record of their progress to be safely preserved. Another aspect of my subject-centeredness is flagged by Lowenfeld and Brittain's suggestion that when one views art as a discipline, "the role of the teacher is seen as a provider of materials."[2] Further, they suggest that in a subject-centered approach, emphasis is given to the correct use of media. According to Elizabeth Delacruz, studies have shown that most of the time in art classes is devoted to teaching students about materials and artmaking.[3] Janet Olson speculates that art teachers have this focus because most of their college courses have been studio based.[4] Wanda May wonders "if the popular focus on studio production and step-by-step routines are utilized by art teachers to reduce the complexity of their work or their students' workload." Perhaps, May goes on to say, "this practice reflects the art teachers' interest in maintaining order as well as the nurturant image they hold about themselves serving the aesthetically disadvantaged masses."[5]

Thus, while some aspects of my teacher-centered approach were consistent with subject- or discipline-centered practices, I had not been aware of the potentially negative effects of my need for control. Elizabeth Delacruz reminds me that teachers' efforts to be structured and organized to accommodate so many children may, in fact, decrease student learning because the child's interests and differences may be overlooked. Stout[6] points out that teaching practice like mine, (trying to

---

2   Viktor Lowenfeld, and W. Lambert Brittain. *Creative and Mental Growth.* 8th ed. (New York: MacMillan, 1987), 28.

3   Elizabeth M. Delacruz , *Design for Inquiry: Instructional Theory, Research and Practice in Art Education* (Reston, VA: National Art Education Association , 1997).

4   Janet Olson, *Envisioning Writing* (Portsmouth, NH: Heinemann, 1992).

5   Wanda May, "Teachers, Teaching and the Workplace," 148.

6   Candace J. Stout, "Artists as Writers: Enriching Perspectives in Art Appreciation," *Studies in Art Education* 40, no. 3 (1999):226-241.

teach as much art material as possible) might result in no learning at all. Like Stout, Cuban[7] argues that students need to be given time to reflect, to question, to probe the significance of, and to judge the validity of ideas in order for serious content to be learned.

As I became more aware of the limitations of my teacher-centered approach, I attempted to grow, which resulted in my efforts to create new schedules for art classes and blueprints for a reconfigured art room. Although these changes never came to fruition, I took some comfort from Cuban's assertion that efforts to change pedagogy towards a more child-centered direction are hindered by the organizational structure of schools. Persons in charge of public school structure determine the teachers' schedules, what to do during "extra" planning time, and in which rooms the teachers will work. Cuban adds that moving to a child-centered pedagogy is also difficult because "teachers have little energy or time during or outside the class to explore ideas with students, to permit students to make errors,… to listen as students try out new thoughts,… or question the teacher's statements."[8] Additionally, as May observes, it is almost impossible for art teachers, especially those working in elementary schools, to get to know their students in any meaningful way due to the scant time they have with them. Luckily, I do have the advantage of a six year relationship with most of my elementary students.

I began to understand that neither a subject-centered nor a child-centered approach is free of problems. Each has its own strengths and weaknesses. Educational reforms in the late 1800s engendered the romantic view of child-centered education. These reformers, known as developmentalists, advocated that schools rely on the natural development of the child to "provide the keys to the riddle of what should be taught."[9] Jeffers points out that years later, Lowenfeld claimed, "art for the child is merely a means of expression and differs

---

7   Larry Cuban, "Persistent Instruction: Another Look at Constancy in the Classroom," *Phi Delta Kappan* 68, no. 1 (1986): 7-11.

8   Cuban, 10.

9   Herbert M. Kliebard, "A Perspective on Twentieth-century Curriculum Reforms," in *Learning and Teaching the Ways of Knowing: Eighty-fourth Yearbook of the National Society for the Study of Education*, ed. Elliot W. Eisner, 1-22. (Chicago: The University of Chicago Press, 1985), 9.

from that of the adult."[10] Eisner explains that a child-centered view, such as Lowenfeld's:

> Starts with the premise that the content of educational programs in the arts is to be used primarily to unlock the potential that each child possesses, that educational content is instrumental to self-realization, and that the first responsibility of the teacher is to know the child well enough to help him develop his own interests and aptitudes.[11]

In addition, the teacher's role was to motivate the children through discussions revolving around them, thereby indirectly assisting in their development. Teachers were sometimes seen as gardeners who were not to intervene in the creative process or impose their own concepts of what is important or beautiful on children.[12] Jeffers points out that this lack of intervention caused concern, because it:

> ...prevented [teachers] from interacting fully, freely, and pedagogically with the child. By the same token, the child is prevented from interacting fully and freely with the adult. Thus, the growth metaphor, as magnifying lens, enables us to see that the Lowenfeldian view of the teacher as facilitator or gardener is also responsible for the adult-child or teacher-student relationship. [13]

Researchers have also found acting as a gardener and not maintaining control results in frustration. Delacruz points out that frustration often comes from the students who want their teachers to manage their classrooms well and to maintain discipline. Moreover, children want teachers to explain things clearly, display interpersonal characteristics, and to act in a fair, friendly manner.

These ideas suggest that a holistic approach in developing one's pedagogy may be more appropriate than moving from one orientation

---

10 Carol S. Jeffers, "Child-centered and Discipline-based Art Education: Metaphor and Meaning," *Art Education* 43, no. 2 (1990), 21.
11 Eisner, *Educating Artist Vision*, 58.
12 Lowenfeld and Brittain, *Creative and Mental Growth*.
13 Jeffers, 19.

to another. In fact, according to Jeffers, many teachers do not prefer either a wholly child-centered or a wholly subject-centered approach. Jeffers contends a comprehensive art curriculum should neither emphasize only media exploration, art elements, and art principles, nor only communication. In *Postmodern Art Education: An Approach to Curriculum*, Efland, Freedman, and Stuhr argue that no one point of view about teaching art should be privileged.[14] Delacruz notes there is an emerging interest in combining child-centered practices with those that are more teacher-centered, thus resulting in a more holistic pedagogy. Holistic teaching, she says, "builds upon research in cognition" and a constructivist pedagogy. It is also "oriented toward humanistic notions of learning, a concern for the integrity of children's realities, and an interest in thinking about and solving the social problems children face." In this model, the teacher becomes a "mentor and expert and is viewed as one of the many sources of information,"[15] not a holder of all knowledge. Motivating students in this approach is done not by the behaviorist practice of conditioning, but by developing projects that are relevant to students' interests and lives.[16]

Delacruz contends that many teachers are not planning with the children's interests in mind and draws from Szekely's view that many art teachers

> ...pre-select the materials, supplies, spaces, themes, and intended outcomes of student work. Criticisms, evaluations, and directions for executing and refining artworks produced in the classrooms emanate almost exclusively from teachers, and students have little understanding of how art teachers come to decide on particular lessons or why prescribed experiences are valuable to pursue. Nor can students say what they have learned from their work or how they would apply their experiences to new works. Most importantly, for Szekely, students have little or no warning about what

---

14 Arthur Efland, Kerry Freedman, and Patricia Stuhr. *Postmodern Art Education: An Approach to Curriculum*. Reston, VA, The National Art Education Association, 1996.

15 Delacruz, 79-80.

16 More recently there has been a move toward a more child-centered approach called Teaching for Artistic Behavior (TAB) in which the child is considered an artist and the classroom becomes the child's studio.

they will be doing before entering the art room, and they spend little time preparing for work, physically, mentally, or conceptually. They simply follow teachers' instructions given at the beginning of lessons. In other words, all the decisions and creative choices have been mapped out by the art teacher. Szekely argues that students should be involved from the beginning in planning their artworks. This includes selecting their own problems to pursue, just as artists set problems to solve. [17]

This discussion shows that there are many approaches to teaching children art. Some are more popular at times than others, but one thing that holds true at all times is that "children of all ages flourish in a loving environment."[18]

This notion of "a loving environment" holds two meanings for me. One is an environment in which my love of art can be shared with children in ways that nurture their own love of art. The other is an environment in which children feel accepted and respected; an environment in which I respond with empathy to their struggles, not just to learn art, but to grow as unique human beings.

---

17 Delacruz, 39-40.
18 Delacruz, 60.

Portfolio Theme

53

Reclaiming Artmaking—Lessons in Empathy

The *Portfolio Artifacts* under this theme portray my renewed experiences as an artmaker. When I began this project, I did not know I would make connections between my own artmaking experiences and those of my students. It was through the cyclical nature of doing an arts-based dissertation that I was able to finally see what I was undergoing in my artmaking process was also what the students might be experiencing.

PORTFOLIO ARTIFACT #9

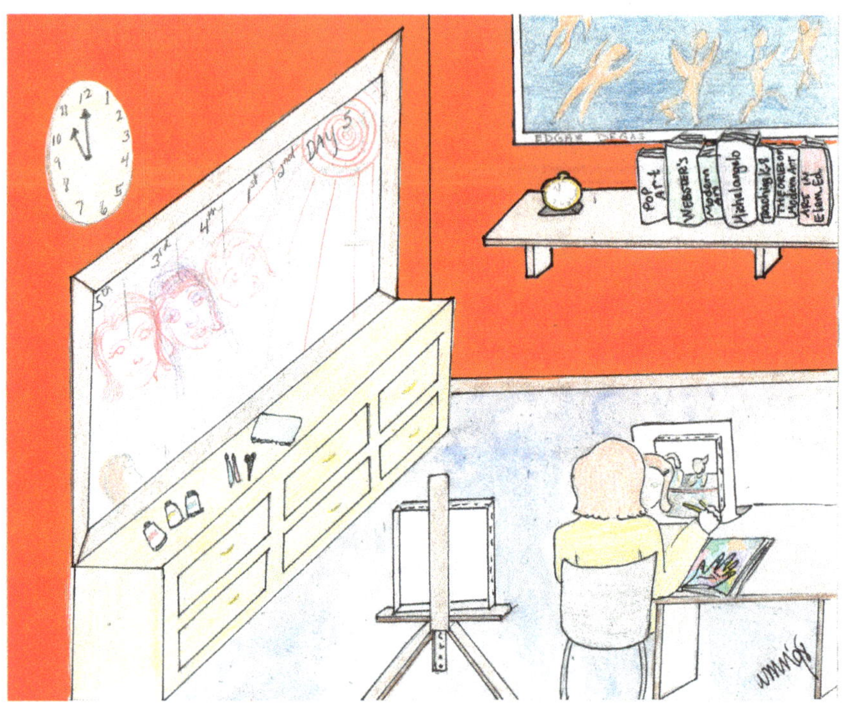

Am I an Artist—Am I a Teacher—Am I Both?

During my undergraduate years, I had been immersed in artmaking. Days and nights were filled with stretching canvases and etching metal plates. When I started teaching, I continued producing art, but more as gifts for others than for personal expression. As weddings, birthdays, and holidays loomed near, I would pull canvases from beneath my bed and quickly paint something to suit a particular living room décor. Occasionally I printed scenes for holiday cards. These held little personal expression. I suppose this may have been a carryover from my college days where I was always given a problem to solve—paint a still life in warm colors; hand build containers based on the theme of a fruit or vegetable (I chose lettuce!). Professors had pre-existing curricula which included problems for novice artists to solve.

Conversely, during my senior year of high school, my teacher had each student select a personal theme to explore and expected us to complete twenty or more pieces by the end of each semester. The high school teacher provided few demonstrations of techniques, and never modeled how to find and solve problems. With this limited understanding, I selected "Animals and Their Habitats" as my theme. Rather than focusing on my beloved pets, I focused on wild life by copying images from photographs in magazines and books. Painting from a photograph was easier than painting from real life, because decisions had already been made about subject, placement, size, and color. Additionally, three-dimensional space was flattened to two dimensions.

Neither the approach of my college professors nor my high school teacher taught me how to find a problem or creatively solve it. I had too much freedom in one case and not enough in the other. On my own after graduation, I moved toward gift-making as a way to satisfy my creative desires, copying from photographs that friends selected for gifts. Eventually, I stopped making any kind of art, which I blamed on my graduate education and my heavy teaching schedule.

As a beginning teacher, I spent much of my day learning student names and preparing supplies for next day's classes. When school let out, I attached student work to display boards and laminated every art print I could find. At home I poured over books and magazines for lesson ideas. Though I was not making art, I told myself that I was still being creative when I wrote lesson plans or made an example for students to view. With no class textbooks to follow, I devoted my energy to writing and executing unique, exciting, and challenging lessons. This left little desire or energy to make art.

In addition to teaching all day, I spent several evenings during my first two years of teaching as a student in a Master's program in General Education. These courses involved reading and writing, not artmaking. Later, in an art education doctoral program, many courses revolved around theoretical, philosophical, and "traditional" research issues in art education. Not until I enrolled in an interpretive inquiry course was I encouraged to draw what I was thinking about my teaching.

Feeling relieved, excited, and somewhat apprehensive, I put pencil to sketchbook for the first time in many years.

Creating pieces of art for my dissertation brought back memories of disappointments and joys related to artmaking. As I renewed my artmaking activities, my student-teacher Heide and I pondered the question, "Are we still good art teachers if we don't make art?" As we shared our opinions, we felt that we were successful art teachers, even without hours of practice in the studio. Despite my years of inactivity, I had received praise from my students and administrators. Indeed, when I demonstrated a technique, the younger students usually clapped or asked, "How did you become so good?" Heide and I continued to wrestle with the question through our sketches and conference conversations. Szekely suggests that our conversations about this issue were important:

> Art teachers come to view the teaching profession not
> as another area of creativity and fulfillment, but as a
> hindrance to personal ambitions. This serious problem
> seldom receives attention in art teacher training or in-
> service education. How to maintain oneself as an artist
> while teaching, or more importantly, how to combine
> art and teaching during one's life needs a great deal of
> discussion and support.[1]

Although Delacruz contends that "many art teachers view themselves as artists,"[2] I have made it a point to call myself an art teacher, because I began working, not as an artist or a teacher, but always an "art teacher." I felt there was a difference, but was not quite sure how to express it. I recalled a painting instructor from my college years. She was well-known in the art world and often exhibited her work. However, as a teacher, she struggled to communicate, motivate, and teach us how to paint. As Kathleen Thompson points out, "producing artists are not necessarily good teachers." Although I was never as good an artist as my painting professor, I felt I had what she lacked—the ability to teach. "The holder of an MFA," Thompson mentions, "is not always a better teacher than one having a degree in education."[3]

---

1   George Szekely, "Uniting the roles of Artist and Teachers," *Art Education* 32, no. 1 (1987): 18.
2   Delacruz, 3.
3   Thompson, "Teachers as Artists," 48.

Patricia Bolanos believes art teachers need a balance between being an artist and a teacher. If the sole focus is on being an artist "little else matters than creating a personal self-expression." On the other end of the continuum, Bolanos says is a teacher who relies on pre-planned lessons and rarely deviates from them. The pre-planned lessons are limited "to self-contained ideas resulting in an in-depth focus on skills which are part of a particular discipline (such as visual art) and limited by it." Bolanos recommends that art teachers blend together their artist and teacher sides to focus on enhancing the creative process for students by synthesizing their artistic and pedagogical knowledge. These kinds of art teachers, she says, have a "significant impact on students and schools." [4]   Rae Anderson concurs, saying that both artists and teachers "are required to know themselves in order to help others know themselves; they both are communicators; and inquiry or curiosity are essential to both practices."[5]

Prior to studying reflective artmaking, I believed I had a positive impact on my students and schools, because no one complained about my teaching and my official reviews were always high. Indeed, I felt changing my practice was unnecessary, perhaps even detrimental, because I thought I had already mastered "the art of teaching art." No one, not even I, noticed my lack of artmaking. Further, as the only teacher in my school with an art education background, I had few opportunities to talk with art colleagues, a situation captured by Wanda May:

> Closing the classroom door or teaching from the trunk of the car may give art teachers a sense of efficacy or autonomy, but this kind of false autonomy does not invite professional dialogue or develop understanding and appreciation of what each individual's contribution is to the total educational enterprise. Professional dialogue is difficult to initiate and foster among teachers. For art specialists, this dialogue is almost

---

4   Patricia Bolanos, "Agents of Change: Artists and Teachers," *Art Education* 39, no. 6 (1986): 49, 52.

5   Rae Anderson, "A Case Study of the Artist as Teacher through the Video Work of Martha Davis." *Studies in Art Education* 39, no. 1 (1997): 38.

non-existent, and teachers' sense of professional isolation is pronounced."[6]

Having the opportunity to collaborate with Heide erased this "professional isolation and led me to wonder if making art would help me to grow as a teacher.

---

6   May, "Teachers, Teaching and the Workplace. ," 147.

PORTFOLIO ARTIFACT #10

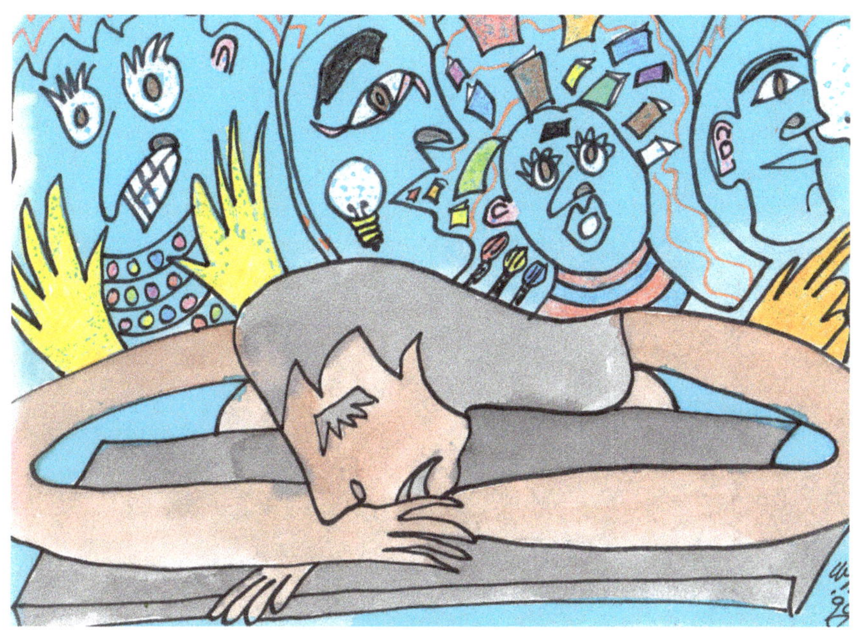

What is "Real Art?"

While perusing our sketchbooks during an early conference, I noticed Heide did not sign her sketches. I thought it odd since I wrote my initials in the bottom right corner of every drawing. Curious, I questioned her reasons, and she said that the sketchbook entries were not "real" art. To her they were merely sketches, not anything she would exhibit. I was confused but chose to say nothing. Not having produced art in many years, I was proud to be making art again, even if some of the sketches were less than stellar. I tried to remember that Heide had just completed four years of college in which she was enrolled in several studio classes per semester. To her, I supposed, a half hour creating sketches five nights a week did not constitute "real" art. I resolved to forget the short-lived discussion and did so until our fourth conference in which I viewed a profile drawing in Heide's sketchbook. She explained that all these simple images we were making were nice but she wanted to do real art that day because the children kept telling her how well she drew. "I just had a need that day to sit down and really do art," Heide said. With that in mind she posed a friend and drew his profile in pencil. Hearing her say this made me wonder again if my simplistic pieces were truly art.

Later, while Heide was teaching, I attempted to do some "real art." Carefully observing the back of a student's hair as it cascaded down her back, I used a charcoal pencil to draw strands of hair, imitating the way it was pulled back with a rubber band. I was grateful the student did not move much because it was difficult to capture the exact angle of her shoulder. Finished I felt that the experience was no different from my other works. In fact, I found the other, symbolic images I had been creating to be more intriguing. I knew it was important to practice drawing from observation to hone my skills, but I also knew that making unique connections with colors, forms, and symbols enhanced my artmaking, so I accepted my simple pieces as works of art. Although the sketches themselves do not rise to the level of "great art," they do represent the best of my thinking about reflection, artmaking, and pedagogical practice at the time of selecting and publically presenting *Portfolio Artifacts*.

PORTFOLIO ARTIFACT #11

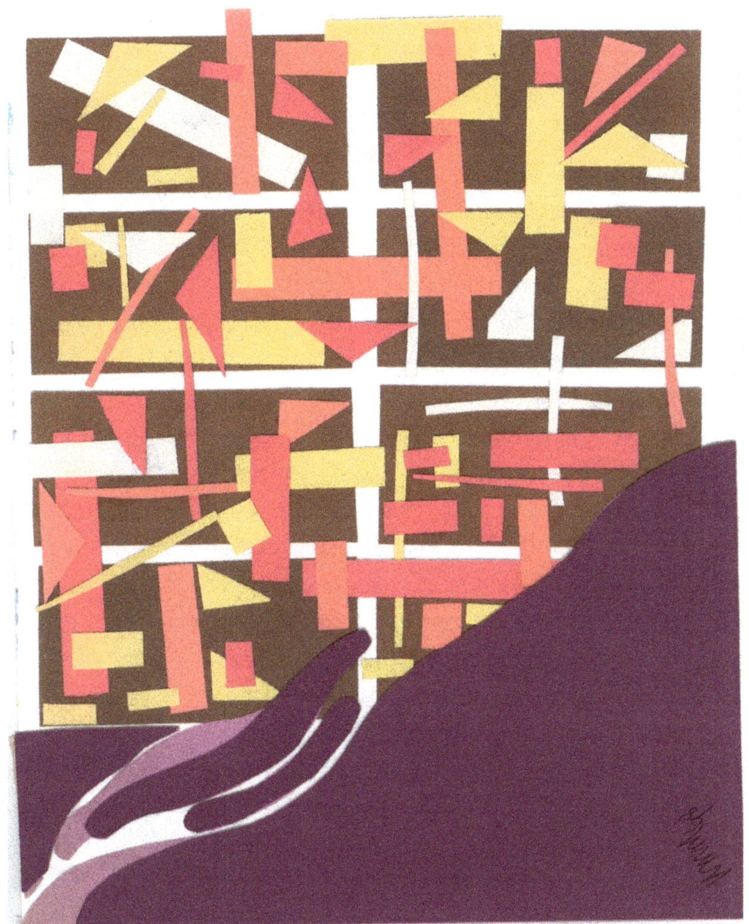

Ordered Chaos

A variety of conflicting emotions arose as I began creating art again. In many instances, I had tremendous fun working with the art media, as I noted in several log entries:

> *Once again the image jumped right into my head. I was unaware of the time, the mess I was making, or even the room I was in.*
>
> *I felt good, relaxed, and pleased.*
>
> *I became one with the pencil and forgot about everything else in the room.*

Such moments are akin to Csikszentmihalyi's description of "flow" when a creator is "so involved in an activity that nothing else seems to matter, the experience itself is so enjoyable that people will do it at great cost, for the sheer sake of doing it."[1] For flow to occur the activity must be balanced, that is, challenging enough for the artist to maintain interest, but not so challenging that the artist is overwhelmed and unable to engage in the activity without extreme frustration.

As much as I enjoyed the sense of flow in my artmaking, I found it gratifying to create lessons that evoked moments of flow for my students, as for example, when my fifth grade students were absorbed in using oil pastels to create a cityscape of a nearby or imaginary town. Watching them, I was torn between roaming between desks and asking them about their work or letting them be. Choosing the latter, I joined in the special moment by making my own art, which fittingly enough, focused on the very pedagogical action I had been pondering. What emerged was "Ordered Chaos," in which I used small rectangles of construction paper to depict the energy in the room. I am represented in the large flowing purple section hovering along the wall debating about what I should do. Sitting at my desk, gluing the pieces, I wondered what the principal or other teachers would think if they walked by and saw me absorbed in my own artmaking. Before I could complete the thought, however, the bell rang, disrupting everyone's concentration. Later, I wrote the journal entry, "*In all my years as an art teacher, I can't think of one time when I sat down during teaching and worked on a piece of personal art.*" Reflecting upon this experience, I was reminded of the power of art to bring an aesthetic order to my jumbled

---

1   Mihaly Csikszentmikalyi, *Flow: The Psychology of Optimal Experience* (New York: Haper & Row, 1990), 4.

thoughts. In creating the brightly colored collage, I brought an aesthetic order to my internal debate about the wisest course of pedagogical action.

Interestingly, another opportunity for me to join my students occurred when Heide was teaching a lesson on additive and subtractive printmaking. I became as excited as the students to start the activity. As soon as Heide finished her demonstration, I eagerly applied colored inks to my wax paper and printed along with the students, who were surprised to see my excitement. Reflecting later, I wrote:

> *I feel comfortable learning from Heide. There isn't a student-teacher relationship anymore. Watching her teach, I jumped up and tried it without thinking about who was the teacher in the classroom.*

During this flow experience, I felt the boundaries between student and cooperating teach dissolve as well as the boundaries between my students and me. As each of us became absorbed in creating our own art, we also became a community in which art was placed at the center. Here the distinctions among teacher-centered, child-centered, and subject-centered pedagogy became irrelevant in our shared space of learning and art-making.

PORTFOLIO ARTIFACT #12

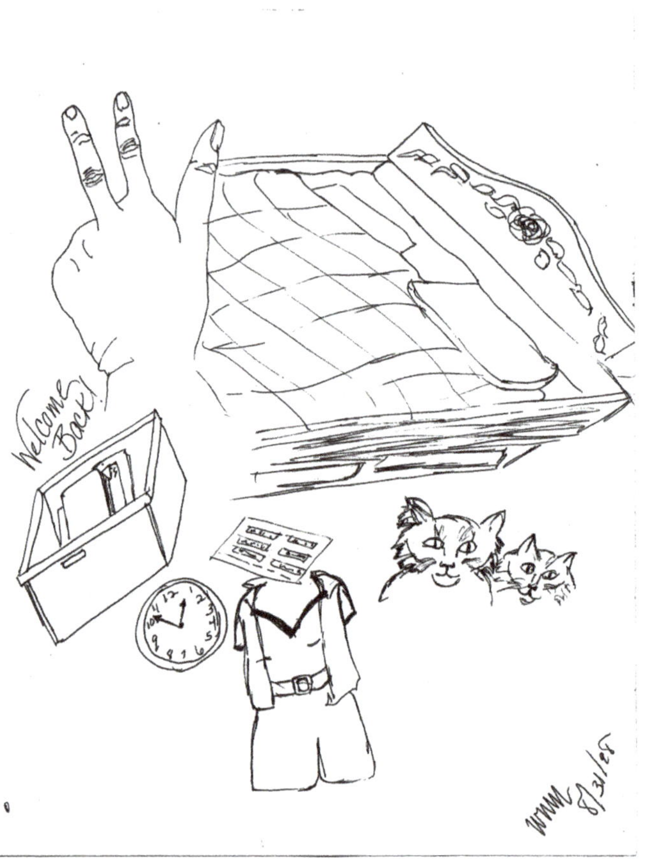

It's Not All Fun

The opportunity to resume artmaking was not all fun and pleasure. Embarking on the reflective artmaking project also engendered pain. On the first day of the project, I stared at the blank pages of my sketchbook, unable to think of any images. I panicked because I had anticipated working in my sketchbook every day. What if nothing came to mind? The symbols I finally drew were frivolous black-line images of my cats, my bed, and a box containing my supplies. The composition is unbalanced and had no apparent connection to anything in my teaching day. Much to my annoyance, on the second day I again struggled for images.

My disgust at the lack of ideas grew when I also had difficulty making them look exactly as I wanted, because my drawing skills were so rusty. In an effort to improve my skills, I drew blind-contour drawings of the students as Heide taught, as well as participated as a learner in some of her lessons. Still, this offered no easy solution to creating meaningful images in my sketchbook.

Weeks later, my principal observed me teaching a printmaking lesson. I decided to make a printed image to represent my thoughts about the lesson which we could then discuss in the follow-up conference. I placed two printed images side by side, and after working unsuccessfully for an hour, I gave up and recorded the following thoughts:

> *I don't like ether image very much. I tried to show four circles for the disciplines and wavy lines representing the raising or lowering of art concepts for each grade level. The original block did not look as good as I wanted it to.*

A week later, still annoyed with the two prints, I made a third. Although slightly improved, it still evoked no insights into my teaching or artmaking processes.

I tried again a few days later. This time, using colored cellophane pieces and markers, I focused on a conference Heide and I had had. The conference was successful enough; the artwork was a blurry, lumpy mess that I almost ripped out of the sketchbook. I curbed this impulse and kept the image as a reminder of what not to do in the future (To this day I discuss this with my students hoping they will refrain from ripping "unsatisfactory" piece from their sketchbooks.) Reviewing the sketch months later, I wrote, *"This shows no insight into my pedagogy, except that you can make artworks that bomb and still go on."*

In yet another journal entry, I merely wrote, *"UUUGGHHH!!!!"* about a piece that began when one of my college students asked,

"Would you send a child to the school where you teach?" Thinking about this question, I weighed the pros and cons, then grabbed some old construction paper, tore it into small organic shapes, and layered them over a page in my sketchbook. Eager to finish, I used a blue permanent marker to write the pros and cons onto the individual shapes. The colors of the paper and maker (brown, pink, green, faded lavender, navy blue) assaulted my eyes; my handwriting looked atrocious.

Although I would occasionally become frustrated with my artmaking, I began to realize that using a sketchbook allowed me to be freer than if I had been working toward a single piece of polished art. I could experiment with collage one day, a marker the next, and whatever media called to me on a given day. Did this freedom allow me to maintain more enthusiasm, I wondered, than I would have had in working on one piece, day after day, using the same medium.

Also looking back, I realized that approaching reflective artmaking as an inquiry process created a pressure to create, whether I wanted to or not. On one hand, the pressure impelled me to do more than I might have been normally inclined to. On the other hand, feeling obliged to create made it difficult to enjoy the experience or to generate insights into my pedagogy. This brings me back to the issue of balance. Too much pressure ends in frustration about making art, but not enough pressure results in far fewer sketches to explore for pedagogical meanings.

Reflective Highlights:
Lessons in Pedagogical Empathy

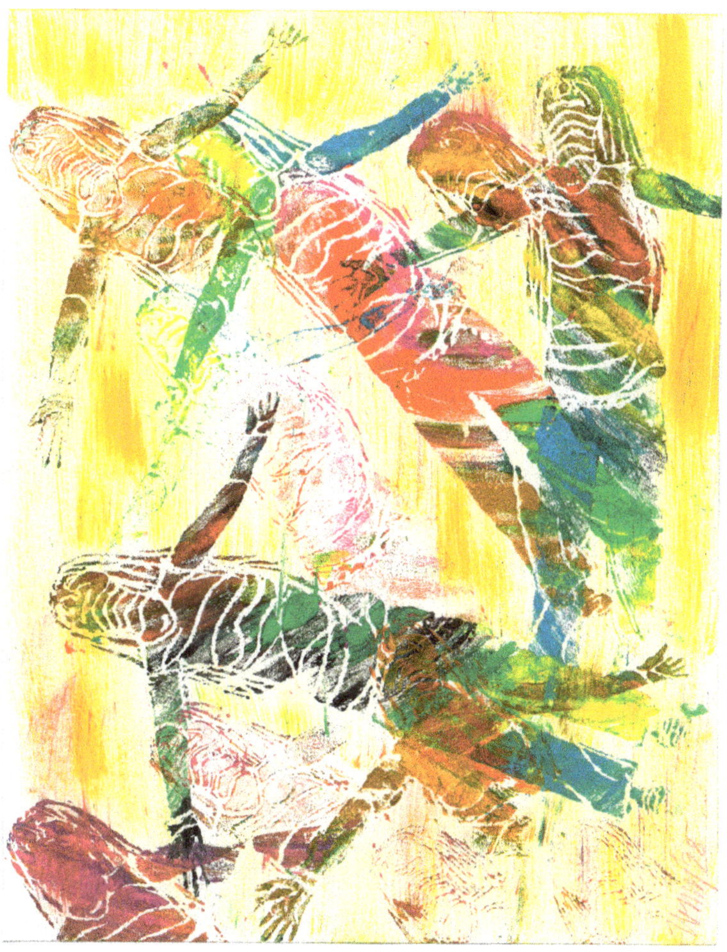

Twenty-seven second graders entered the room one afternoon, full of questions about what we were doing. I told them a two-week lesson about emotions was planned. In my lesson plans I had written that students would hear a story about feelings, observe their faces in mirrors as they took on the appearance of various emotions, and begin to draw themselves looking mad, scared, happy, sad, etc. As

I started the lesson I guided them to look into the mirror and switch emotions as I called out various feelings. I'd call out, "Now, let's see proud. Okay, embarrassed next!" I placed two sheets of white paper at their spaces as they decided which pair of emotions they wanted to use. "Okay everybody; draw the outside shape of your face. Is your chin smaller than your forehead? Are there curves, any straight lines? Look closely and draw what you see. I know some of you are not finished but let's begin cutting these out now."

As an early finisher collected paper scraps from the floor, others still worked carefully to cut out their shapes. "Sweetie, you have to move along or we'll never get done," I whispered to Elaine, who typically was the last to finish any activity. Her neighbor, Doug, however, raced through everything. When asked to observe each feature carefully before drawing it, Doug set his pencil down in three minutes. His face lacked eyebrows and his nose was shaped like a triangle. So I told him to look again to see what his face really looked like. Ten seconds later, he put his pencil away, folded his arms across his chest, and talked to Derrick three tables away. Derrick, too, was done, but his angry pose was quite stunning with scrunched up eyes, twisted nose, and a mouth snarled in anger. I had no real suggestions for him, but since seven minutes still remained, I told him to work a bit more on the shape of his eyes. Elaine was still painstakingly trying to make her two eyes the same size as the clock ticked down. "Okay, everyone, we'll glue on the hair next week and use the faces to act out a story. See you next time!"

This vignette illustrates a typical lesson for me. The children usually responded well to these types of lessons, and since most seemed able to complete the activities, I did not worry about the ones like Elaine who were slower than the rest. In fact, I did not think much about the children's actual experience in the art room until much later when I examined the artifacts in my sketchbook.

One aspect I noticed was that each entry in my sketchbook took a different amount of time to create. The subject of the artwork determined how much time I needed, not the clock. There were intervals when I was able to capture my thoughts in ten minutes, while others, like "Ordered Chaos," took two or more hours. The tiny rectangles and squares used in that sketch required a lot of patience since I wanted to place them in specific spaces to emphasize the creative energy the students were exuding that day. Other entries could be completed more quickly. I sensed when a piece was finished to my satisfaction, and no amount of time would make it better or communicate more of my thoughts and feelings.

I could also sense which medium would convey the meanings I wanted to portray. For instance, September 23 was a particularly bad day, when I observed a new fifth grade student acting silly and uncooperative when Heide asked the students to pose for a figure drawing. I admonished the "new girl" to let her know this behavior was not acceptable in *my* classroom. She reacted by giving me a curt reply and a blank look. Later another student talked throughout my instructions, disrupting the entire class. Already primed by the new student's response, I reacted hastily by yelling and moving his seat to the back of the room. During the next class, a student deliberately tore another student's pocket. By this time, I was livid. I took both "offenders" into the hall and yelled loudly, giving them no chance to explain. They began to cry, and I felt like joining them. The remainder of the day followed in the same vain with more talking and confusion.

I vented my frustrations in my journal entry for the day:

> *Each class seemed to have someone misbehaving. It was as if each class played off of one another—making me crazy. The roots in the sculpture penetrate into one another in an attempt to represent this behavior. I probably became more sensitive to the outbursts since they kept recurring class after class. I reacted quicker and sterner with each incident. I had little patience by the end of the day. As I began rolling twisty coils for the roots, I noticed my fingerprints embedded in the clay—perhaps indicating my influence on their (mis)behavior. The tiny spheres and fringes show the intricacies of each child's life and what they are bringing to the classroom that I have absolutely no idea about. Writing and creating are causing me to remember that these kids are coming to school with a lot of problems. I've always wanted the art room to be a place for them to relax and leave those problems*

> *behind. Instead I reacted to their behavior in a way*
> *which added to their problems. I also recognize that I*
> *came to school frustrated about an added class in my*
> *schedule. So I had other frustrations that I might have*
> *been taking out on the kids.*

Trying to capture my feelings in my sketchbook, I selected oil pastels, feeling the layers of color would smear over one another, just as the problems in the classes have layered on top of each other. The drawing, like my day, began badly, so I abandoned it and searched for another medium. During that evening's college course, I asked the students to mold a sculpture with clay. While they worked, I kneaded a piece of clay, a motion that almost seemed therapeutic. As I relaxed and let go of the stress from the day's events, I decided this would be a more appropriate medium to capture my thoughts and feelings. The next day, I twisted and molded clay into a sculpture; weaving and looping coils over one another into a piece I called "Out of Control."

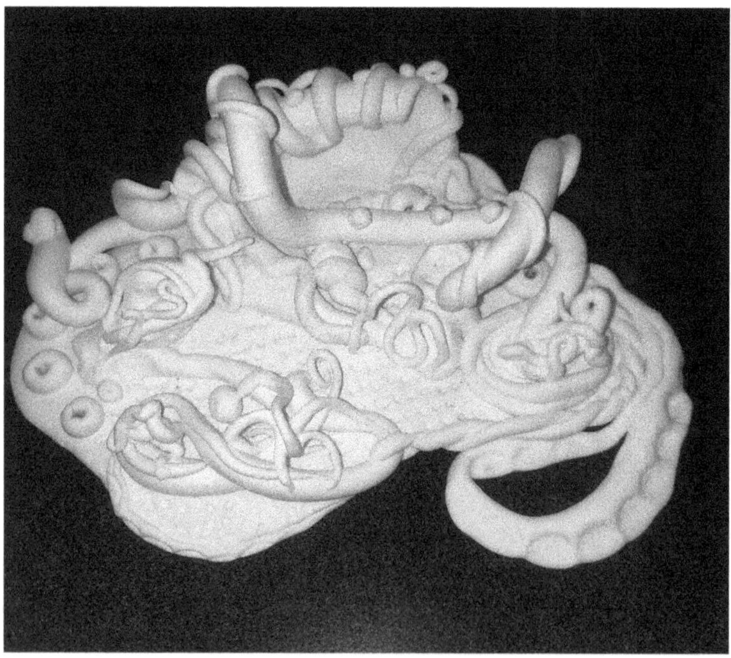

There have been other occasions when I have reacted hastily to students without ever wondering why I responded as I did. Creating and writing about the sculpture led me to see that I, too, was contributing to the commotion in the classroom. Was I in a sour mood? Did I yell because a student rubbed me the wrong way? Was I ignoring someone because the previous class was talky and disruptive? Through the sketchbook, I was able to look beyond my reactions toward the underlying reasons. When I did so, I saw that my bad mood, not the students' behavior, had been the source of the problem. Being told I was going to have two additional 40-minute classes added to my already heavy teaching load caused resentment. I went to sleep angry and woke up annoyed. Although I was in a foul mood that particular day, I failed to remember that children also have bad days. Having grown up in a happy home with few problems, I tended to forget that so many children have difficult, even hellish, lives. Molding the sculpture reminded me of this and helped me to make a more concerted effort to respond more positively the next time I encountered an "unruly" child or disrupted class.

Over the seven weeks that Heide and I engaged in collaborative artmaking, I immersed myself in creating quick sketches or laboring more slowly with other pieces. For the first time, I felt I had a reason to create art. No instructors were telling me to make heads of lettuce or complete twenty paintings before the semester ended. I was finally in charge of my own ideas, and though it was difficult to identify problems, I welcomed the challenge. The pieces I created were not for exhibit, nor were they for someone's living room wall. They were made for me to gain insights into my own teaching, and whether the insights were pleasant or not, they still had significance for me. Reading in the arts-based educational research literature, I was struck by a passage that exemplifies my artmaking experience:

> An artist seeks to understand something about the world, about self, about materials and ways of making expressive forms. Engaging with materials, thoughts, and feelings, an artist participates in a search. This search to bring something into being requires attention to details, a sense of relatedness among all parts within a whole, and tolerance for the tension of not knowing

what will emerge. Through the practice of creating
expressive forms and experiencing a depth of meaning
and value in the process, an artist develops and refines
affective, intuitive, aesthetic, and relational ways of
knowing. Knowledge internalized through experience
of engaging in creative process is a key value that an
artist can bring to educational research.[1]

Likewise, discourses in art education have suggested that making
art enhances teachers' ability to understand and empathize with their
students' creative endeavors.[2] This parallels calls in the art education
community for art teachers to create art themselves. As Feldman
reminds us, an art teacher

> …must be able to see his or her subject through the eyes
> of the students; this calls for pedagogical empathy, the
> ability to imagine that you are a student encountering
> the body of materials, tools, techniques, and ideas in
> the person of an enthusiast.[3]

Janice Rahn feels that when pre-service teachers are asked to reflect
upon their own artmaking they can "begin to empathize with the learning
processes of young people."[4] Additionally, Kathleen Thompson, an art
teacher who ceased creating her own art at the beginning of her career,
indicates if art teachers were to produce art on a regular basis they
could identify with their students as they involved themselves in the
"processes of conceiving and expressing ideas for use in artworks."[5]
Thompson noticed when she delved only into the theoretical side of

---

1   Carolyn Jongeward, "Visual Portraits: An Artistic Approach to Qualitative Educational
    Research," Paper presented at the Annual Meeting of the American Educational Research
    Association, Chicago, IL, April 1997.
2   See for example Anderson, 1997 and Feldman, 1988.
3   Edmond B. Feldman, "Clay: Arguments for and with. Proceedings of the Symposium: The
    Case for Clay in Art Education," reprinted from *Studio Potter* 16, no. 2 (1988), 21.
4   Janice Rahn, "Autobiography as a Tool in a Teaching Environment and Studio Practice,"
    in *Women Art Educators IV: Herstories, Ourstories, Future Stories*, ed. Elizabeth J. Sacca
    and Enid Zimmerman, (Bourcherville, Quebec: Canadian Society for Education through Art,
    1998), 135.
5   Thompson, "Teachers as Artists," 48.

creating, she forgot about the pain and pleasure that occur when actually making art. Based on years of teacher observations, Patricia Bolanos believes that art teachers who make art are better able to "articulate their own creative processes and the meaning of art work, as well as to teach the creative process to others."[6]Wix reminds us, "artmaking is a unique way to tell one's story" and encourages art educators to use these stories of personal artmaking to "educate students about their own artmaking processes."[7] Mortimer so strongly believes art teachers need to create that he proposes school districts provide release time for art teachers to pursue artmaking.[8] Thinking about these ideas in relation to the structure of my lessons, my students, and my own artmaking experiences I began to see patterns. Were the students feeling the same way I did when their artwork failed? How did they feel when the bell rang, and they were not finished? Did others' talking distract them? Did they need more time to experiment? Were the problems I selected relevant to them?

Arthur Efland contrasted "child art" to "school art." The former is "a spontaneous, unsupervised form of graphic expression usually done outside of school by children for their own satisfaction or in response to a need felt in an environment other than school."[9] In contrast, the latter "tells us a lot more about schools and less about students and what is on their minds." Efland describes the look of school art as predetermined by teachers—often classroom, rather than art teacher. They select the theme, medium, and length of time necessary to create a product. Under the worst of circumstances teachers may resort to "photocopied worksheets, pre-cut paper collages and sculptures, and holiday art."

Since I made it a policy to select the medium for my students, I was surprised to hear Efland call this a restriction. I defended my reasons for selecting the media in a number of ways. First, by varying the media used for each lesson, I would prevent the students from becoming bored or defeated by one particular medium. Second,

---

6 Bolanos, 51.

7 Linney Wix, review of *Art and Fear: Observations on the Perils (and Rewards) of Artmaking*, by David Bayles and Ted Orland. *Studies in Art Education* 39, no. 3 (1998): 281-284.

8 Andrew Mortimer, "Approaches to the Teaching of Critical Studies," in *Critical Studies in Art and Design Education*, ed. David Thistlewood (Portsmouth, NH: Heinemann, 1991), 57-70.

9 Efland, "The School Art Style: A Functional Analysis," 37.

frequently changing media would expose students to a variety of skills and techniques which, I rationalized, is appropriate at the elementary level. As an artmaker, however, I recognized how my choices might restrict the students' artmaking processes. As a result, I began to shift my pedagogy, teaching techniques in several media and allowing students to decide which would best suit their creative needs.

In my "school art" approach, I not only chose the media students would use, I also determined what problems would be of interest to them. Once again, discourses in art education contradicted my preconceptions:

> Teachers must allow students opportunities to define aesthetic problems for themselves and to set their own goals. Students will not be well equipped to face a blank canvas if their educational experience has consisted primarily of doing teacher assigned projects. They need to have opportunities to exercise their skills in organizing, analyzing, creating, integrating, and evaluating to solve aesthetic problems.[10]

Reflecting on my emotions lesson for the second grade students led me to look beyond the surface assumption that I was creating opportunities for students to be creative and productive, and to wonder whether I was actually restricting their creativity by pre-selecting the problem for them to solve. It seemed I was mirroring my own college artmaking lessons where instructors defined problems for me. Over time, I relied on my professors to provide the problems, and when this structure disappeared, I lapsed into making gifts, and eventually, nothing. Was my problem-setting approach discouraging students from making art after leaving school? As Roland contends:

> ...if teachers want children to be more thoughtful
> and understanding about art as adults, they need to
> provide them with opportunities to act upon their

---

10 National Art Education Association, *Visual Arts Education Reform Handbook: Suggested Policy Perspectives on Art Content and Student Learning in Art Education* (Reston, VA: NAEA, 1995), 10.

own intellectual initiative as often as possible in
their art classes at school. When all of the decisions
are made for them, students may fail to see art as a
cognitive activity intrinsically valuable to pursue or
as something meaningful to their lives in and out of
school. In order for students to construct meaningful
views of art, teachers need to increase their sense of
personal control over their own thinking and learning.
This is likely to occur if teachers: (1) permit students,
at least occasionally, to formulate their own problems
to solve; (2) offer them meaningful choices to make;
(3) expect them to monitor and evaluate their own
thinking; (4) help them see the value in what they are
doing; and (5) encourage them to become actively
involved in the learning process.[11]

Delacruz argues that for students to engage in meaningful inquiry
in the art room, the teacher must center the instruction around teaching
students how to find and solve aesthetic problems. Eisner recommends
that art teachers talk to students to get their input on writing the
curriculum rather than assuming to know what they like or dislike.
Janice Rahn advises art teachers to assist in motivating students by
suggesting ideas but refraining from providing the theme. As she
says, "There is no better way to have students discover something for
themselves than to re-view experiences through critical reflection."[12]
When Carolyn Thompson interviewed students about their feelings
about art classes, many reported that "the problems imposed by their art
teacher as universal assignments failed to address their own pressing
concerns and too often erected barriers along the paths they had
chosen."[13] Students also described their experiences as "superfluous,
irrelevant, and unchallenging." These comments reminded me to seek
student in-put about interests and thoughts. Incorporating these into my
lessons helps students practice finding and solving aesthetic problems.

---

11 Craig Roland, "Improving Student Thinking through Elementary Art Instruction," in *Art
    Education: Elementary*, ed. A. Johnson (Reston, VA: National Art Education Association,
    1992), 30.
12 Rahn, 135.
13 Thompson, "Experience and Reflection," 17.

By not involving myself in artmaking, I also forgot what it was like to experiment with a new medium, perhaps resulting in demanding that my students watch a demonstration and then begin their project immediately with no experimentation. Printmaking with Heide and the fourth grade students allowed me to understand what it was like to work in a medium I had not previously used. When I created the additive print, I discovered my ink dried too quickly and what resulted was a pale impression of my original image, thus reminding me of my own students' failures with various media. Kathleen Thompson recalled how "stupid" she felt when she began learning to macramé and used this memory to reassure her students that learning a new technique can take a long time. Thompson's recollection and my own experience with additive printing remind me of problems that students might encounter in using new media and help me to help them work through those problems.

As my empathy increased, I began to understand how students might feel when I rushed them to complete their projects or told them to work longer on a piece because the class was not over. As Conant observes, art cannot "be turned on at 8:35 a.m. each Monday, Wednesday and Friday and turned off 50 minutes later."[14] Likewise, Leeds says, "the continual fragmenting of seemingly disconnected subject matter into short time spaces through which we process students, teaches them to not get deeply interested in anything, as it will be taken away from them in just a few minutes."[15]

In many instances during my personal artmaking I completed a piece rapidly whereas other pieces required more time. If I had been forced to work on some sketches longer, they might have looked better, but I might also have resented spending more time on them than I wanted to, or I might have overworked them to the point of ruining them. If I had to stop working on a piece before I considered it finished, I tended to have less enthusiasm and drive than when I had first started. I could now imagine that students might also have a difficult time regaining their enthusiasm for an incomplete project after a week-long break.

---

14 Howard Conant, "Season of Decline," in *New Ideas in Art Education: A Critical Anthology,* ed. G. Battcock (New York: Dutton, 1973), 45.

15 Jo Leeds, an interview by Julia Kellman, "The Voice of an Elder. Jo Leeds, Artist Teacher, A Personal Perspective on Teaching and Learning," *Art Education* 52, no. 2 (1999): 45.

Surely, they were mystified as to what they should do when I told them to work longer on a piece they were done with (either because it was finished or their interest was exhausted).

I also gained greater empathy for the students who, like those Thompson interviewed, did not like "art making on demand":

> They seemed to know that it was, in some ways fundamental and unforgivable, a violation of the artistic process. Yet they continued to long for someone who could help them along their way, who could challenge them to move faster and farther and offer a hand to steady them when they faltered. [16]

Creating art for personal expression does seem to require different lengths of time, but for many artists, time restrictions are a real part of their world. Since many make a living by selling their work, artists must live by the patron's clock. If they are commissioned to paint a portrait, the customer will expect to have the work in their hands on a specified date. When artists plan to exhibit their pieces, specific deadlines must be met. Artist Arthur Ganson says he gives himself time restrictions because he feels he was spending too much time on some works. The restrictions, he discovered, led to interesting and pleasing results. So, in an odd way, a 40 minute class period may prepare those who may become future artists for the time restrictions imposed upon them. Of course, not all (or even many) elementary students will pursue art careers where time restrictions become an issue.

Efland suggests that when teachers select the theme, medium, and deadlines for students, they are essentially "commissioning" a work. The teacher as "client-patron" is "the dispenser of rewards for commissions completed within specifications."[17] As a "dispenser of rewards," I often found myself lacking. "The Praiser" depicts a colorful image of me raising my head and arms to the sky, awaiting praise, which shines down in vertical yellow streams. The image came about as I recalled my primary-aged students demanding attention from me as I distributed supplies. As I quickly passed their tables, they would hold

---

16 Thompson, "Experience and Reflection," 17.
17 Efland, 41.

up their pictures and ask, "Do you like mine?" Without much attention, I nodded and mumbled, "Yes, it's fine," to all who asked. I responded similarly when Heide asked me if I had liked a lesson she had just taught. The question faded from memory as the next class entered the room, but it resurfaced later during a conference. Printing "The Praiser" was a reminder that we all need praise, specific praise, not a casual affirmation of "it's fine." I thrive on praise and probe to learn exactly what was good about me or my work. The sketch of "The Praiser," therefore, represents my needing praise, but also the importance of reciprocating with specifics when praising others.[18]

Repeatedly giving perfunctory responses, ignoring students' requests for feedback, or criticizing work may increase students' feelings of vulnerability. Bayles and Orland point out, "in making art you lay bare a truth you perhaps never anticipated, that by your very contact with what you love, you have exposed yourself to the world. How could you not take that criticism of your work personally?"[19] If we wish to have students communicate their life experiences through making art, we must also be "prepared to help them with the fears around that. This assignment of supporting students in the act of artmaking is crucial to art education."[20] Paraphrasing David Pye's comments in *The Nature and Art of Workmanship*, Andrew Mortimer says, "the teacher/ artist is undoubtedly the best person to make children aware of, and share, the possibility of failure that comes with the creative process."[21] Suggesting possible improvements and allowing students to take or leave them seems to allay some of their fear and foster trust.

Thompson reports that her high school students seemed to have greater respect for her when they learned her work was being exhibited. Noticing this change in her students had the unexpected effect of increasing her own self-esteem. I experienced something similar when I gave each of my fifth grade students a sketchbook and invited them to create any images they wished. To encourage them, I explained that

---

18 I was reading over this passage in the Fall of 2020, when I had a new student teacher. It reminded me to give her very specific, timely praise as she learned about becoming an art teacher.

19 David Bayles, and Ted Orland. *Art and Fear: Observations on the Perils (and Rewards) of Artmaking* (Santa Barbara, CA: Capra Press, 1993), 38.

20 Wix, 281-284.

21 Mortimer, 64.

I, too, would be drawing in my sketchbook about the events of my teaching day. I showed them my sketches and felt the students seemed impressed with my work. Adam asked, "How did you do that so nice?" I was proud to say honestly, "Because I practice." I hoped our shared involvement in artmaking would prompt the students to feel more open to discussing their ideas and to ask about my work. Perhaps my adventures in artmaking will keep me mindful of the limitations of "school art" and more encouraging of "child art."

In order to create a productive "child art" pedagogy, I need to find a balance between too much freedom and too many restrictions. I had been overwhelmed by the number of choices open to me in high school and had lacked strong enough command of techniques and media to explore unique solutions to problems. Marme-Thompson points out that "true freedom occurs when choices are made within a structure that is stable, reliable, and protected from distraction."[22] Eisner points out that, "To expect students to learn entirely new skills and at the same time cope effectively with the aesthetic and expressive aspect of their work is to expect a great deal."[23] Conversely, the excessive control I experienced in college fostered a reliance on instructors to find the problems for me, and by prescribing the media, theme, and time limits, helped me to solve the very problems they had designed. Therefore, in striving for a balance within my own pedagogy, I keep in mind Eisner's observation about Discipline-Based Art Education:

> No door can be opened without a curriculum having both structure and magic. Without structure in our curriculum, we get no automaticity. With no automaticity, we get no internalization. With no internalization, we get no magic. Those who worry about the deadening potential of structure, I hope, will be reassured that those of us committed to disciplined-based art education are also committed to magic. Without it there is no art. Without structure there is no access.[24]

---

22 Christine Marme Thompson, "What Should I Draw Today? Sketchbooks in Early Childhood," *Art Education* 48, no. 5 (1995): 11.
23 Eisner, *Educating Artistic Vision*, 163.
24 Eisner, "Structure and Magic," 25.

Revisiting my "artist-self" deepened my understandings of the ways in which artmaking processes for my students can be hindered or enhanced. The first of these understandings relates to the issue of time. As I worked in my sketchbook, I often entered a state of flow in which I became unaware of time and let the media and/or theme guide me. Students, too, need this experience in spite of the arbitrary limitations created by the 40-minute class structure. A second understanding relates to the importance of making time to talk with students about their interests and involving them in decisions about the curriculum. A third understanding is the importance of giving children opportunities to select their own media. Finally, it is essential that I remember my role as an elementary art teacher, for as Carolyn Thompson says:

> …it is relatively easy to supply materials, demonstrate techniques, and dictate approaches to art; conducted at this level the teaching of art is no more complicated than the teaching of any complex skill, such as tire changing or ballroom dancing. It is far more difficult, more demanding and decisive an experience, however to attend the birth of meanings, the emergence of form. In the latter case, it is the presence of the teacher, not mastery of technique that is essential.[25]

Presence, of course, entails more than merely occupying the same space. It requires careful attention, openness to the concerns of others, empathetic understanding, and a willingness to affirm the efforts of my young art-makers.

---

25 Thompson, "Experience and Reflection," 27.

Portfolio Theme

A Posture of Listening

The *Portfolio Artifacts* clustered under this theme revolve around patterns of listening: listening to myself as a teacher, listening to my elementary students, and listening to my student teacher. The thoughts depicted in these pieces also extend my reflections on the *Portfolio Theme of Control and Freedom.*

PORTFOLIO ARTIFACT #13

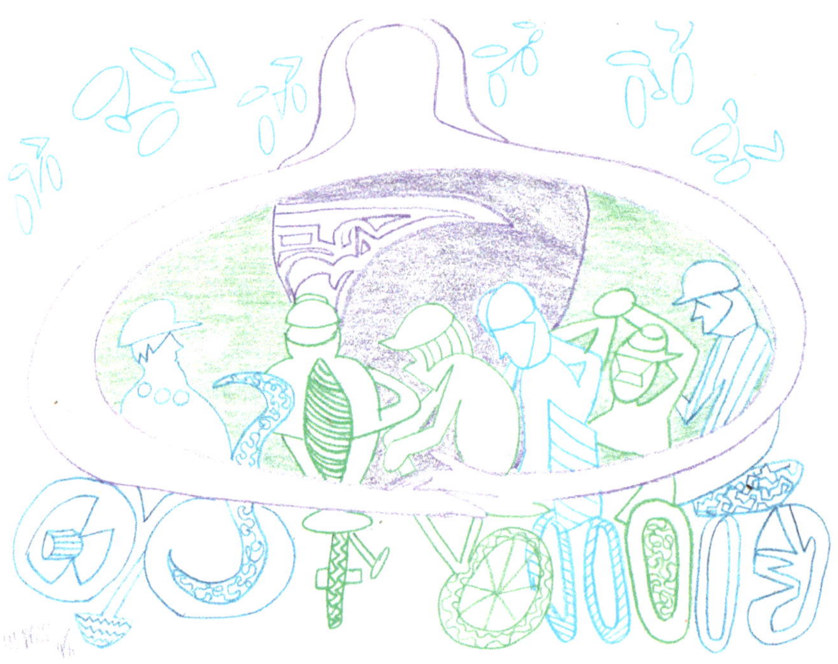

Good to See You

On the third day of school, I left concerned once again that I had no unique visual images swirling in my mind. I headed slowly down the hallway, feeling discouraged and trying desperately to think of something to draw. Carrying my sketchbook out to my car, I encountered a group of six, middle school boys riding their shiny mountain bikes through the parking lot. Having been in my classes for five years, they rode toward me, wearing surprised smiles, apparently pleased to see me. I was just as pleased to see them and returned their smiles and waved a big hello. I chatted with them about their summer, their bikes, their new art teacher, and what they were learning in art class. Knowing I had to get to the local college for my next teaching responsibility, I regretfully started to say goodbye to "my kids," but they begged me to stay for a few more minutes to watch them jump over a small ditch they had built in the dirt at the end of the parking lot. Standing to one side, I waited nervously as each one leapt into the air and landed safely on the grass. I clapped enthusiastically, and with a pang of sadness, said good bye, knowing such chance encounters would be rare.

Although our talk lasted only a few minutes, it had an impact on me. I wondered about the rapport I had built with these boys. What had happened in our five years together that made them feel comfortable enough to stop, talk, and beg me to watch their biking stunt. These jumps were most likely reserved for their own private boyhood moments, not for an adult to witness, especially a teacher who might tell them they should not be jumping on school property. What about our relationship made them think I would react positively, even enthusiastically, to their seemingly dangerous activity?

Our conversation and my questions prompted me to draw "Good to See You," which depicts a caring, fun-filled relationship based on our moments together in the art room. I began with a large, curving, deep purple outline to represent my reaching out and embracing these former students sitting on bicycles. Next I filled half of my figure with a deep purple as a way to represent the warmth I felt seeing and talking with them. In some ways I felt as if they were still my students, because I had watched them growing up over five years. The cool colors represent the calm and comfortable atmosphere as I listened intently to their stories. Although the air was filled with teenage energy, the moment was somehow peaceful, demanding a cool color scheme. The simple, geometric shapes of their bikes and helmet-clad figures reflect the brevity of our conversation, but the detailed, swirling patterns inside the outlines indicate the depth of meaning this seemingly trivial conversation had for me. Lastly, I added the leaping bikes along the top of the sketch to show their desire to perform for me. Finishing, I wrote, "It was good to see them."

PORTFOLIO ARTIFACT #14

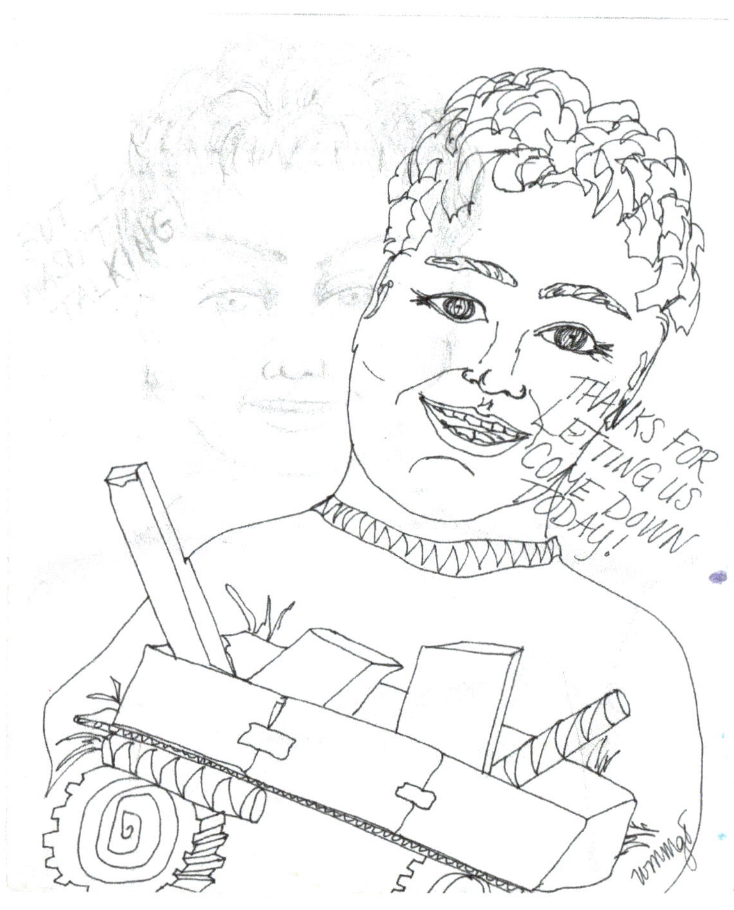

From Crying to Smiling

The sketch "From Crying to Smiling" depicts a shift in my relationship with Scott, a student I had judged as "troublesome." Scott had arrived at our school a year before I started my reflective artmaking project. He was disheveled, unruly, and loud. I repeatedly told him to be quiet, but it did no good. I tried to ignore him for most of the year, so I was startled (and embarrassed) when he walked into class the last day of school, carrying a painting on a large piece of old wood. "Here Mrs. M. I made this for you," he said proudly. Not knowing what to say or what to do with the splintered panel, I told him I would place it in my home. Instead, I haphazardly leaned it against the wall in a back corner where it languished forgotten for the summer.

The following year Heide joined my classroom, and Scott reappeared as loud as ever. The day Heide taught her lesson about copper masks, Scott's voice rose above the group, and gritting my teeth, I fumed, "Isn't he ever going to learn what is expected of him?" Raising my own voice, I warned Scott that I would move his seat if I heard him talking out again. Two minutes later I heard him asking someone for a pencil. Although that was a legitimate request, he was so loud I felt compelled to carry through on my threat. "To the back, Scott, right now!" He stood and tried to explain, but I refused to listen. "Move it!" He failed to hide his tears as he picked up his supplies and move to the back of the room. For the remainder of the class I could hear him sniffling.

In reflecting on my encounter with Scott, I was embarrassed by my reaction. The next week I deliberately greeted each student, including Scott, with a smile and comment. During the class, instead of ignoring Scott as I had been doing, I talked with him about his ideas for an invention. Grudgingly, I had to admit that he had a pretty clever idea and maybe he wasn't so bad after all. In fact, his voice didn't seem as loud, and he seemed to be working harder. Pushing my earlier impressions aside, I attempted to get to know him better.

Several weeks later, Scott asked if he could come to the art room at the end of the day to get some last-minute supplies for his invention. Alone in the room, Scott showed me pieces of wood and wire he had brought from home. His father had even bought him a battery to move a lever on the contraption. As Scott selected several wrapping paper tubes, he blurted out that his mother moved away when he was in first grade and he rarely saw her. I was impressed with his creativity, ingenuity, and was excited that he was so engaged in the activity. At the same time, I was saddened by the information about his mother.

Picking supplies, he noticed his painting in the back corner of the room and, instead of asking why it wasn't in my home as I had said, he just exclaimed, "Cool! There's my painting!" Soon his bus was called, and he left with a loud, "Thanks for letting me come down today!" This time, rather than telling him to lower his voice, I smiled. Guilt about my previous attitude towards Scott lingered, but I was pleased our relationship had grown from anger and tears to respect and smiling.

That night I sketched "From Crying to Smiling." I started by lightly drawing Scott's crying figure in pencil and overlapped it with a black outline of him smiling to represent my change in attitude. The notes accompanying the sketch described how my misconceptions about Scott changed when I took the time to listen to him. The drawing reminds me that my need for control had caused me to punish rather than listen. As I began to examine my relationships with other students, I continued to sketch and write. The next Portfolio Artifact depicts a particularly painful realization.

PORTFOLIO ARTIFACT #15

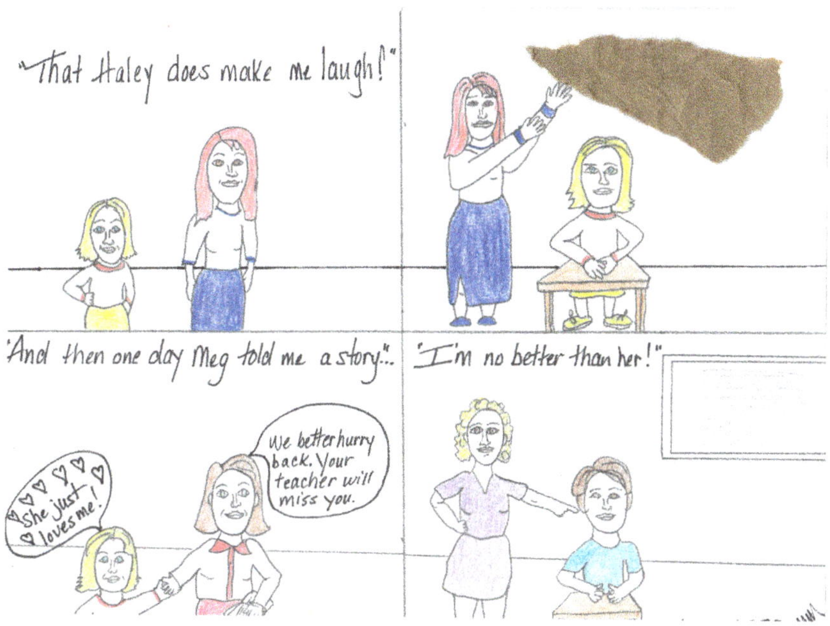

That Haley does make me laugh!

This sketch emerged from a conversation I had with Meg, a close teacher-friend about a student named Haley. Haley was new to our school, and she never, ever, stopped talking. Standing on morning bus duty, I would hear her talking as she hopped down the bus steps. In addition to her incessant chatter, she would throw tantrums if she were reprimanded. Even a "teacher-look" would cause her to wail.

During our conversation, Meg whispered, "That Haley sure does make me laugh!"

"Haley?!? You mean that talky new girl who always pouts and cries if you look at her funny?" I asked incredulously. "How in the world does she make you LAUGH? She's horrible."

Meg chuckled and described a time when Haley was running late, which meant Meg had to escort her to her next classroom. As they walked, Meg commented, "I'd better get you back to your teacher or she'll wonder where you are."

"I know," replied Haley. "She just loves me so much."

That afternoon, Haley walked into my room, chattering away. The minute I heard her talking during instructions, I let her know this would not be tolerated. The usual tantrum erupted, and I took her into the hallway to let her know who was the boss. Returning to the room with a dramatically sobbing Haley, I commented to Heide, "I'll never know why Meg likes her. I'll never be able to even tolerate her behavior."

While thinking about my day as I drove to college, I kept hearing Meg say how Haley makes her laugh. I respect and admire Meg. She and I have similar teaching styles and similar views of students like Haley. So I was surprised and puzzled that Meg could see something good in Haley, while I could not. This brought to mind another student named Louis, whom I liked, but his classroom teacher did not. His teacher constantly complained about him in the faculty room and reprimanded him in front of others, including his peers. She nagged at him regularly and called his mother practically every day. I have met a handful of teachers like that in my work as a substitute—teachers who seem to take pleasure in exerting their power over children they deem to be behavior problems. I felt superior to these types of teachers, because I never "picked on" students. Yet, that night, I realized my reactions to Haley were as terrible as those of Louis' teacher. I was deliberately planning to let Haley know in no uncertain terms who was the boss each time she came to art class.

My collage that evening was a three part illustration done in the style of a children's book with cut-out sections for people's faces. The cover depicts Meg and Haley happily walking hand-in-hand down the hall. Their faces change into my stern face staring down at a crying Haley. Flipping the page my face "morphs" into the type of teacher who nags students, and Haley's face becomes Louis'. The caption at the top reads, "I'm no better than them!" The exchange with Meg allowed me to see a nasty side of myself. I ended the cartoon-like book with the question, "The end?" in the hope that this entry would remind me of the teacher I could become if I were not careful. After that evening, I instantly "see" the drawing whenever I hear Haley's chattering and try to listen to see if what she says will make me laugh.

PORTFOLIO ARTIFACT #16

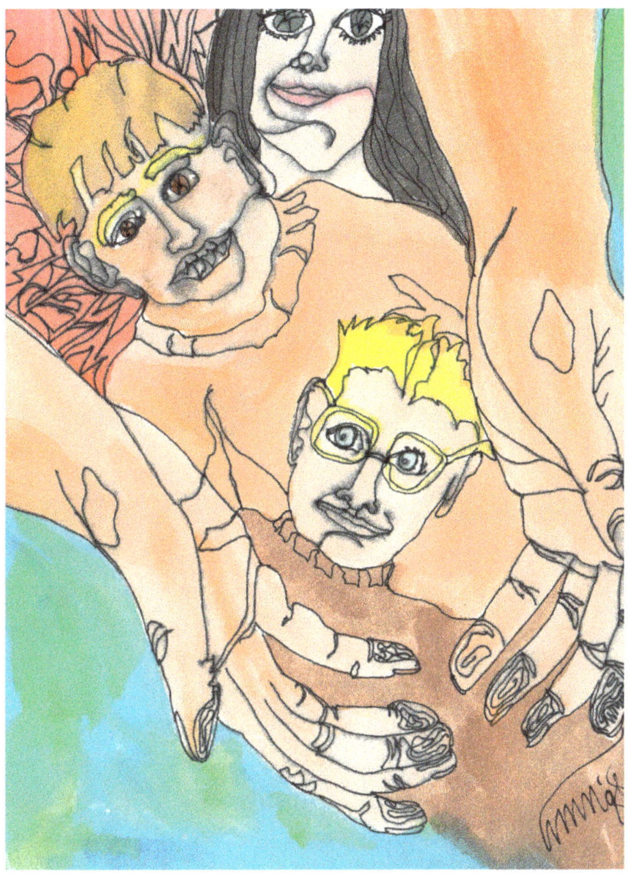

Safe Haven

As I continued to reflect on my relationships with students, I became concerned that I was now looking only at my imperfections. I knew I was not always the miserable teacher I was sketching in "From Crying to Smiling" and "That Haley does make me laugh." To gain a more balanced perspective, I began to search more consciously for moments when I made children feel at home in the art room. When three instances came to mind, I created the abstract, "Safe Haven," using a fine black marker first and then a wash of watercolors. Three students are depicted inside the gentle embrace of my hands.

Kay appears in the upper quadrant because of a brief moment when her large hazel eyes met mine at the end of a class on drawing self-portraits with chalk pastels. When one student said he wished he'd had more time to work on his picture, I agreed and said I wished all of them could stay in the art room all day. Kay's eyes lit up, and looking straight into mine, nodded in agreement. In that instant, I knew she would choose to be in the art room creating all day, every day. She usually lingered after class to help clean up or put last minute touches on her drawings. She borrowed many art history books from the library and asked if she could be on a team which studied Picasso since she had a deep interest in his work. I loaned Kay various art supplies she want to experiment with and suspected Kay would grow up to be an artist.

Donald rests diagonally under Kay. Donald was an unusual boy who physically reacted with violence towards teachers and classmates. A variety of trigger points could set him off, and no one could figure out when and why these outbursts occurred. I warned Heide about Donald, but added that he never erupted in art class. When Heide asked why, I recounted the following story.

> One day Donald arrived for art earlier than the rest of his class. He was angry and refused to sit in his seat despite my repeated requests to do so. I was feeling a little desperate and wondered if he would attack me. He was making nasty face and glaring at me each time I told him to sit down. I had talked with Meg about Donald, and she said she would like to make faces back at him. Remembering this, I decided to try it. Facing Donald I contorted my face into the silliest pose I could imagine and stood waiting for a response. He stared back, startled to see a teacher acting so oddly. I rearranged my face again, mimicking his movements. Luckily, he began to laugh heartily, and so did I. When his classmates arrived, they found us both giggling.

From that moment on, I never had a problem and never
had to make faces with him again.

One afternoon when Heide was teaching the class, Donald entered
and asked, "Where's Mrs. M?" I wrote these words surrounding
Donald's head, because I was touched by his seeming to miss me.
"How sweet," I wrote, and felt good that for at least some children, I've
created a warm, safe environment.

Louis, his eyes full of hope behind his glasses, awaiting to hear a
kind word, is the final face in "Safe Haven." Coincidently, a student
in Louis' class also mentioned wanting to stay longer. I repeated my
earlier wish that students could stay all day, while looking straight at
Louis to see his response. He, too, nodded and said quietly to me that
he would like to stay in the art room all year. Sadly, I told him I would
love to have him there all year, but for now he had to leave. He smiled
and quickly headed out the door, probably afraid he would be in trouble
if he were the slightest bit late.

Using markers, I drew the three portraits and chose to surround
them with my hands as if I were creating a special, perhaps safe, space
for these children. The gesture of my hands is reminiscent of the ones
in "Good to See You" and is a contrast to the gesture in "Hands Down."

I added fingerprints to represent the positive influence I had had
on these students. Somehow I have left my imprint on them. The
red words, "Where's Mrs. Milne" flow around Donald's head while
the other colors merge into one another creating a blurry, peaceful
environment; one I have attempted to create for each of these children.

Reflective Highlights: Mutuality in Relationships

The patterns in these *Portfolio Artifacts* deal with the subtheme of mutuality. In "Safe Haven" Kay and I shared a mutual love of art. Kay seemed to recognize and identify with my passion for all aspects of art. Her deep interest in art at such a young age reminded me of my early affinity for art. During the five years I taught Kay, we talked of little else besides art when we were together.

Donald and I had a different type of relationship—one of mutual respect. I respected his anger and his space. Rather than meeting anger with anger, or trying to control him, I responded with humor through which we came to a mutual agreement.

Louis and I had a mutual dislike of teachers who embarrass their students. Though I did not tell him this, I made it a point to talk quietly and respectfully to him.

In examining these patterns, I began to connect my actions and reactions to the students' and use this information to begin designing an environment in which all students could feel safe. Yet, there were further lessons about mutuality that I still had to learn.

Portfolio Theme

93

Collaborative Artmaking

As an only child, I feel comfortable working alone. This inclination was reinforced by an educational system which focuses on individual student learning and accomplishments. The *Portfolio Artifacts* in this theme trace my growing appreciation for collaborative artmaking with a colleague and among my students.

PORTFOLIO ARTIFACT #17

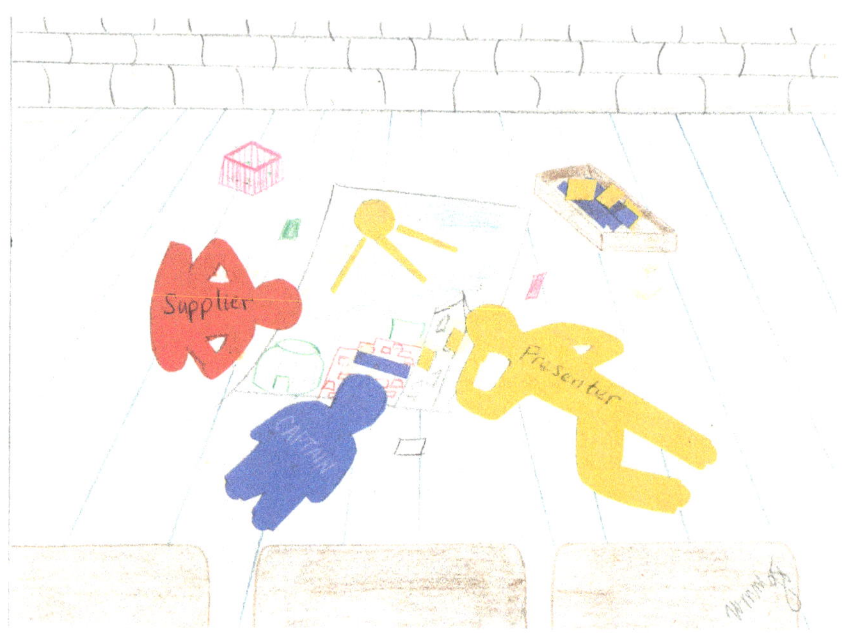

Cooperative Cities

"Cooperative Cities" exemplifies a fundamental shift that occurred in my thinking about artmaking. I begin with incidents when my controlling teacher-self did not fully appreciate the value of children working together.

Paul and Linnie sat in the front corner of the room working to complete their enlarged flower drawings Paul had been absent during one of the days devoted to this activity, so he was busily trying to complete the background in his picture as I called out, "Ten minutes left, everyone. This is the last day to work on your flowers." As I roamed through the room, I arrived at Paul's desk where Linnie was helping him to fill in the solid red, oil pastel he had chosen to complement the green shades in his picture. They must have noticed the annoyed look on my face and started explaining. I interrupted their stuttering and asked Linnie not to work on Paul's art. This was his creation and no one else should touch it. Later they told me that Linnie had noticed Paul's desperation to finish, so when she offered to help, he handed her a crayon which she began using to fill in the corner of the paper nearest to her.

Paul and Linnie's cooperation was not the first or only time I noticed students working on each other's projects. Two third graders, for example, decided to connect their papers, forming a large landscape depicting their neighborhood. Another day, a student was layering many colors of tempera paint into her sky. Her neighbor watched intently as the colors mixed and finally took her own brush and added some green to the sky. Although the first student did not seem to mind, I immediately said, "Please don't paint on her picture." Perhaps I stopped these actions, because some students get very upset if someone else touches their picture. Others get angry if they think their neighbors are copying their ideas. But I think it goes deeper than that for me.

I had always viewed artmaking as a personal, unique, and independent experience. As a student, from kindergarten through graduate school, I rarely was asked to work on a group project. I assumed working together on an art piece was cheating. The school culture reinforced this attitude of independence and competition. After all, the grades I received did not mention anything about how well I worked in a group.

Several years into my teaching, I participated in a staff development workshop about cooperative learning and began to see the value of this method. Accordingly, I began to develop a few cooperative learning units in which students made a mural or engaged in group critiques. Usually, however, I reverted to independent projects.

When Heide joined me for her student-teaching experience, I wanted to show her what a collaborative project looked like, so I pulled out a mini-unit plan I had done in previous years. The unit began with students designing an imaginary city on 24" x 36" white poster paper. I then asked students to select a tag from a box; each tag listed a specific job such as art supplier, group reporter, and project captain. I was surprised to see that no one got upset about their job selection and seemed to take their role very seriously. As the children got to work, I circulated through the room, listening and watching as the cities emerged. Stopping by one group I asked, "What kinds of ideas are you coming up with?" I laughed out loud when Nick said, "Good ones!"

That night I created the mixed media sketch, "Cooperative Cities." In the piece I emphasized the importance each job had in the success of the lesson. In reflecting on this piece, I said the following:

> *This project reminded me how much fun it is to work cooperatively. They weren't arguing. Last year when I taught the same lesson and did not give them any specific jobs, it wasn't nearly as successful because they kept tattling on one another. I thought it would be the same, but the jobs improved the lesson tremendously. They were on task and seemed to be very proud of their work.*
>
> *When they were working, it seemed like it just didn't matter if any group was mixed. I mean you couldn't tell who were the Learning Support students or the "regular" students; none of the kids were complaining that someone was ruining their work. The students who were mainstreamed really got a lot out of it.*
>
> *I felt so good about this lesson, because it showed me this is a viable way to teach. I want to continue using cooperative ideas. I never liked doing collaborative art projects much before this.*

Although I saw the benefits of group artmaking, it was not until I worked with Heide that I fully experienced the joys of creating together. As Heide's time with me drew to an end, we decided to collaborate on a piece that would depict our thoughts on reflective artmaking. As we brainstormed, we drew from our sketchbooks and notes to create a tri-fold collage "book." This experience was delightful, not only because I had the experience of making art with a colleague, but also because I had someone knowledgeable about artmaking with whom I could talk. Working side-by-side with Heide, her ideas became a springboard for my own and vice-versa. As we created, we generated so many ideas that at times we were overwhelmed with possibilities. What a contrast to the lonely nights I had had trying to draw just one image. In spite of the many calls for cooperative learning in the art education literature, it took my immersion in the process to fully appreciate both the pleasure and the depth of learning that can occur through this pedagogical approach.

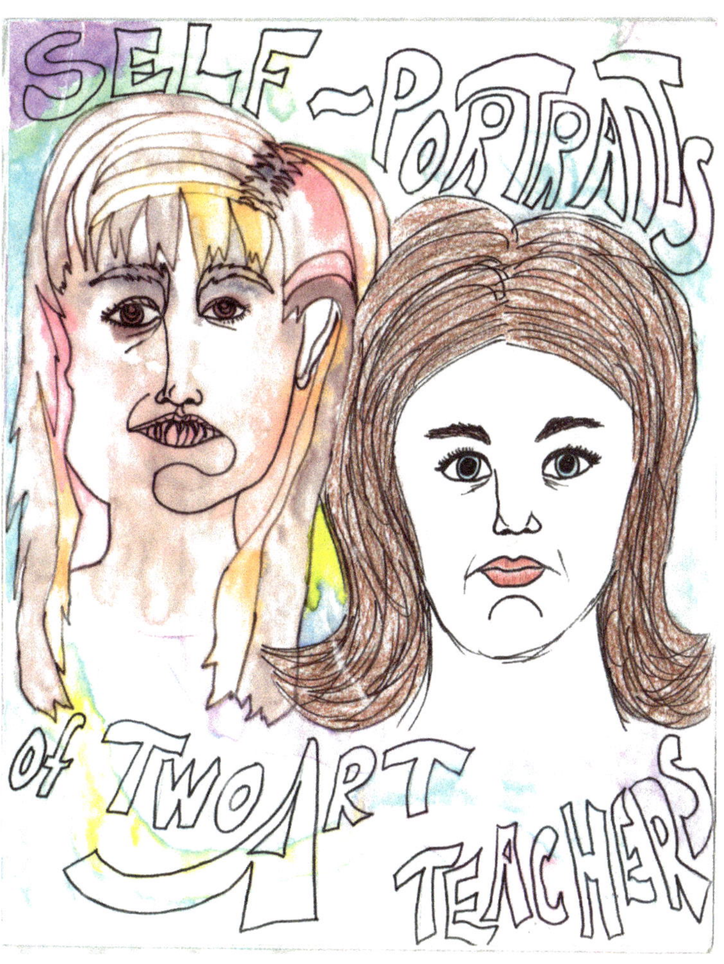

PORTFOLIO ARTIFACT #18

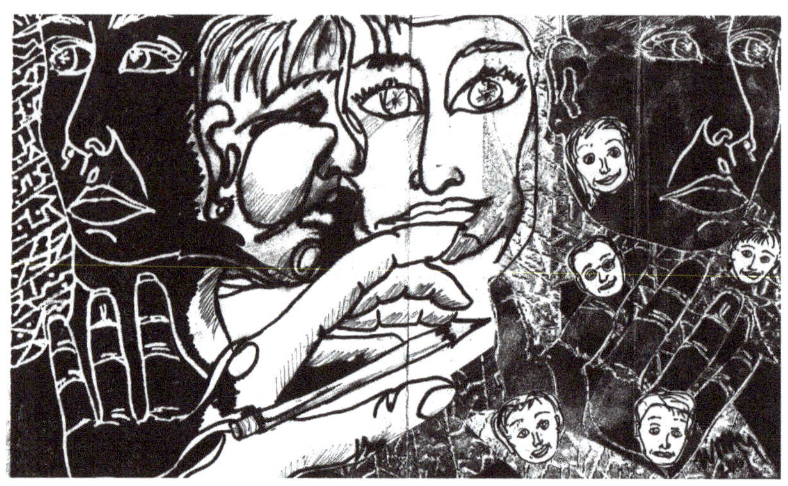

Transformation

Crafting the *Portfolio Artifacts* helped me to see commonalities between my students and me. When I finally got past my annoyance with the chatter and loud voices, I was able to discover mutual interests as I took time to listen to students. Finding these points of connection paved the way for more trusting relationships to develop. The following highlights weave together relevant discourses with issues of listening, building rapport with others, collaborating and sharing the meaning of art work, and perhaps most importantly, teaching as a lifetime of study.

Parker Palmer suggests that looking at oneself can be one of the most important things a teacher can do for herself and her students, because listening enables the teacher to come to know herself. When Palmer began to reflect on his own pedagogy, he found that teaching came from inside himself:

> As I teach, I project the condition of my soul onto my students, my subject, and our way of being together. The entanglements I experience in the classroom are often no more or less than the convolutions of my inner life. Viewed from this angle, teaching holds a mirror to the soul. If I am willing to look in that mirror, and not run from what I see, I have a chance to gain self-knowledge—and knowing myself is as crucial to good teaching as knowing my students and my subject.
>
> In fact, knowing my students and my subject depends heavily on self-knowledge. When I do not know myself, I cannot know who my students are. I will see them through a glass darkly, in the shadows of my unexamined life—and when I cannot see them clearly I cannot teach them well. When I do not know myself, I cannot know my subject—not at the deepest levels of embodied personal meaning. I will know it only abstractly, from a distance, a congeries of concepts as far removed from the world as I am from personal truth.[1]

Palmer suggests teachers find ways to "talk to themselves" in order to get to know themselves more fully. I began to "talk to myself through artmaking and discovered fears and worries as well as strengths. Through the creation of "That Haley does make me laugh," I began to view myself as someone I did not like or respect. Without the self-examination, however, I may have continued unaware on the path to becoming that hated self, because as Palmer says, "we teach who we are."

Through examining the artifacts in my sketchbook and journal, I came to better understand my students. Donna Livingston says successful art teachers reflect, monitor, analyze, and evaluate their

---

1   Parker J. Palmer, "The Heart of a Teacher," *Change* 29, no. 6 (1997): 15.

teaching.[2] Drawing and talking about my sketches helped me to hear my students' hopes, desires, and dreams.

Listening to students and responding to them takes time and often requires a pause in my usual thinking. My inclination to rush through the work in a 40-minute class resulted in my responding hastily, or worse, ignoring all together what the students were saying. As Eisner reminds me, caring relationships take time to develop, but this time is well spent because it makes schooling educative. Mutuality develops as teachers better understand students and students better understand their teacher.

During my explorations, I recalled the words of a high school art teacher, Ken Cutway, who spoke at one of my graduate classes. When talking to his own students, he habitually reminds himself to pause before speaking and ask himself, "Is what I am about to say going to build our relationship or break it down?" I had forgotten my desire to emulate this teacher, but the reflective artmaking process rekindled my commitment to build rapport in this way. Now when I hear Haley's chattering, I see my sketch and pause to consider what response will precipitate a tantrum or contribute to a better relationship. As with Haley, my earnest attempts to pause before responding to students sometimes falters, but my commitment to change has been reinforced through the positive responses from my students.

When I finally saw the importance of listening to myself and my students, I realized students like to work together. This change in perspective led me to authors and artists who also create in groups. Quiltmaker Rita Irwin observes that there has been a shift from artists who create alone to those who participate in an "interactive, interdependent, dialogic collaborative." By listening for long periods of time, Irwin says that she and her fellow quiltmakers began to "appreciate the depth and complexity of our acquired understandings." "Our aesthetic partnership developed," she goes on to say, "through a listeners' paradigm. We learned from one another and came to collaborative decisions."[3] Irwin and her fellow quiltmakers recommend that others

---

2   Donna Livingston, "Highly Accomplished Art Teachers," *A National Arts Education Advisory.* Alexandria, VA: National Arts Education Association. Fall, 1999.

3   Rita Irwin, "Listening to the Shapes of Collaborative Artmaking," *Art Education* 52, no. 2 (1999): 36, 38-39.

collaborate through artmaking by placing listening at the center of their art, rather than the visual. By permitting and encouraging my students to create with a partner or team, I may discover more about them, and they may discover more about me.

Sharing my sketches with students was another way in which I began to establish rapport. The act of sharing seemed to engender a new level of engagement as they asked: "What was that one about?" "What did you make that out of?" "Do you have any other drawings to show us?" During my second year of having students create their own sketchbooks, our sharing was more open-ended. I asked questions similar to those the students asked leading to conversations I had previously not considered valid art experiences. As we shared our art products and processes, I was able to hear another level of the students' thinking. Merely observing them had not allowed me to hear their frustrations or their joy as they mixed paints or discovered a "new" color. Even when I had asked students to write about their processes I had selected the questions. Things like: "What was the hardest part to do and why?" "How would you do this project differently?" When students critiqued famous pieces of art, I also selected the questions or guided their conversations in ways I thought best suited them. Talking in a seemingly casual manner about our artwork brought forth new insights into my children's thinking about their art. As Simpson says:

> ...becoming sensitive to what learners know from experience, and what they bring with them to art class is invaluable to teachers. Teachers with this information about their students can make planning choices that will allow students to participate fully in a lesson. The idiosyncratic nature of learners can be exploited in the artroom, rather than be considered a managerial problem.[4]

Another artist-teacher, Lisa Schoenfielder shared her personal art work with her high school students and found, instead of sarcasm or ridicule as she had anticipated, her student reacted positively to her very

---

4   Judith Simpson, "Constructivism and Connection Making in Art Education," *Art Education* 49, no. 1 (1996): 58.

personal difficulties in conceiving a child. Although Schoenfielder does not recommend that every art teacher expose their personal problems to their students, she does feel that, in her case, the students began to see her as "human being who experiences hopes, dreams and even sadness just like they do." She adds that in encouraging students to "look, interpret and critically question their own and other's works of art, they were able to share what matters to them, as well as listen to each other's concerns."[5]

Similarly, artist-teacher Martha Davis told observer Rae Anderson[6] that artists do not have to share their art with anyone if they choose not to, but it is necessary for art teachers to share their work with their students if they want to really teach.

As Heide's teacher I discovered that sharing our artwork ended in a more open, trusting relationship. Although feelings of vulnerability emerged, we were able to relate to one another better than if we had not shared. Before leaving for her next assignment, Heide gave me a framed quote done in calligraphy:

> The teacher said to the students :
>   " Come to the edge."
> They replied : "We might fall."
> The teacher again said :
>   " Come to the edge."
> and they responded : " It's too high"
>
> "COME TO THE EDGE"
>   the teacher demanded.
>
> And they came,
>   and she pushed them.
>   And they flew.

---

5   Lisa Schoenfielder, "Artist's Statement," in *Women Art Educators IV: Herstories, Ourstories, Future Stories*, ed. Elizabeth J. Sacca and Enid Zimmerman (Boucherville, Quebec: Canadian Society for Education through Art, 1999), 150-151.
6   Anderson,. 1997.

I reflected on this time with Heide to understand that, even though she is an adult, aspects of our collaborative artmaking can be incorporated into my elementary teaching, despite the associated vulnerability. Sharing art with Heide, opened a new avenue for incorporating dialogue with my students into my pedagogy.

Reflective Highlights

Leeds reminds me "learning to teach, like learning to be an artist, is a lifelong proposition... Really outstanding teachers always march to their own drummer, and the cadence is seldom like anyone else's."[7] As I listened, watched, and pushed myself to the edge and beyond, I have discovered ways of teaching that have worked and others that have not. Edmund Feldman, writing in *Art Education*, advises that to avoid burnout, teachers need to:

> ...grow a little bit during every teaching encounter. The teacher should go into each class with the expectation that he or she will come out stronger and wiser...If you want to end your career on a high instead of a low, then concentrate on becoming a better teacher of art. That's where the greatest possibilities of growth are...that's where you are largely in charge of what you do; that's where the satisfactions outweigh the pains; and that's where you associate yourself with some of the most remarkable men and women who have ever lived.[8]

Adams says a "teacher affects eternity; he can never tell where his influence stops"[9] and Day adds:

> The bond between teachers and learners is a timeless bond, essential for human progress. In a sense, teachers are immortal. Our influence is endless, as learning is passed from generation to generation. As teachers, we are given the opportunity to bless the lives of others, to share what we believe is virtuous and good, and to make their lives richer and better.[10]

---

7 Leeds, 46.

8 Edmund B. Feldman, "Best Advice and Counsel to Art Teachers," *Art Education* 46, no.5 (1993): 58-59.

9 Henry Adams, *The Education of Henry Adams* (Boston: Houghton, 1918/1973), 300.

10 Michael Day, "Art Education for the New Millenium," Keynote speech presented at the Annual Convention of the National Arts Education Association, Chicago, IL, April 1998.

Delacruz echoes these views, saying, "the way an individual teaches informs students not only what he or she thinks about art but also what he or she thinks about them."[11]

Although Adams, Delacruz, and Day emphasize the positive influence teachers can be in a student's life, I am aware that it can be negative as well. Listening to and looking at myself through artmaking, listening to students through shared conversations and artmaking, observing students as they work independently and cooperatively, and finally, sharing my artwork with students—all of this helps to build trusting, more positive, and possibly, more creative pedagogical relationships.

---

11 Delacruz, "Design for Inquiry," 4.

REFLECTIVE ARTMAKING IN PERSPECTIVE

Looking Back

Throughout the cyclical phases of reflective artmaking, both positive and problematic issues arose. These issues, it seems to me, have implications for other teachers who might wish to engage in reflective artmaking. The *Portfolio Artifacts* under this retrospective theme highlight these issues.

PORTFOLIO ARTIFACT #19

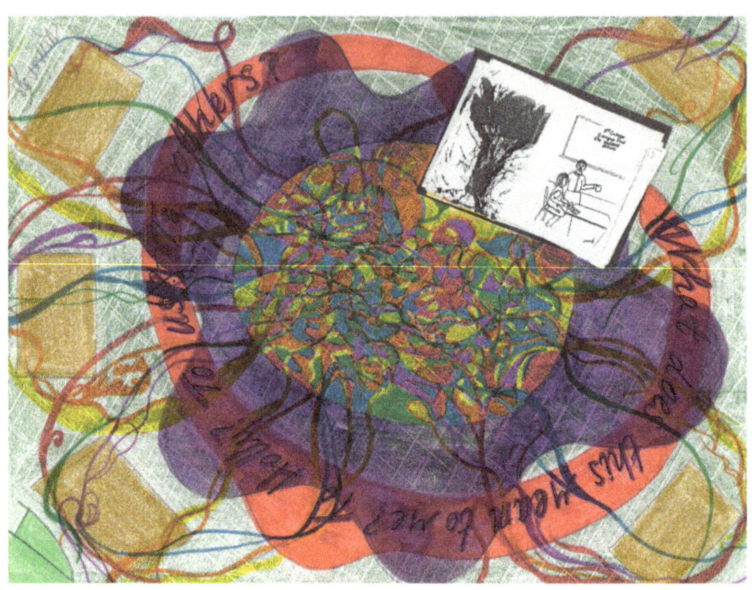

Finding Time to Reflect

Prior to engaging in a study of reflective artmaking, I was vaguely aware that I did not make time to create art or to reflect. My avoidance stemmed from a variety of legitimate reasons including lesson planning, teaching at both the elementary and college level, home life, and creating art displays at school. Initially, I thought embarking on this study would not entail much time or energy. This soon turned out to be quite wrong.

I was constantly trying to carve out small amounts of time in my day to work in my sketchbook. When inspiration struck as I was teaching, I couldn't simply stop my lesson to record my thoughts and feelings. *Finding Time to Reflect* depicts such a moment when a third grader asked an intriguing question, but I was in the middle of explaining a technique and organizing the children into groups. When the class left, I had forgotten the question that had so intrigued me. I considered documenting my teaching by videotaping my classes. This idea quickly fell by the wayside when I contemplated the impossibility of watching thirty or more tapes per week.

Interestingly, my most creative ideas came at inconvenient times as I was driving, showering, or teaching. Yet, when I set aside a specific time to work in my sketchbook, I had difficulty generating ideas I wanted to portray. Both at home and at school, I resented not being able to draw immediately and capture my thoughts while they were fresh (and before they evaporated from memory). At home, mundane interruptions included the phone ringing, my husband, the need for sleep, and a variety of household chores. At college, although I made a point of arriving early or staying late, my drawing time was interrupted by students wanting to chat—even though I had closed the door and shut off the lights. I took some consolation in the fact that the lack of time for reflection during the teaching day is apparently a common condition.[1] Finding even 30 minutes to do a sketch and jot down notes was not easy when managing an overloaded schedule.

A greater challenge arose as I began to conceptualize the meanings embedded in my sketchbook, log, journal, and conference notes. No set formula could guide my thinking. The only option was to immerse myself in the artifacts and the literature I was exploring. In the end, I spent about eight months repeatedly reviewing and rereading the artifacts as I began to identify thematic elements I wanted to portray. Although this period of intense reflection gave rise to some of the most meaningful insights into my pedagogy, the time commitment might be too burdensome for those under no obligation to engage in a formal inquiry. That said, I believe there is still a value in creating reflective artifacts of practice. In those early stages, I regained my desire to make art, and I found problems I wished to solve visually. Additionally, working in the sketchbook was therapeutic, giving me an appropriate avenue to vent my frustrations.

---

1 See Jackson, 1968; Posner, 1993; Rogers, 1985. Full citations in Bibliography.

PORTFOLIO ARTIFACT #20

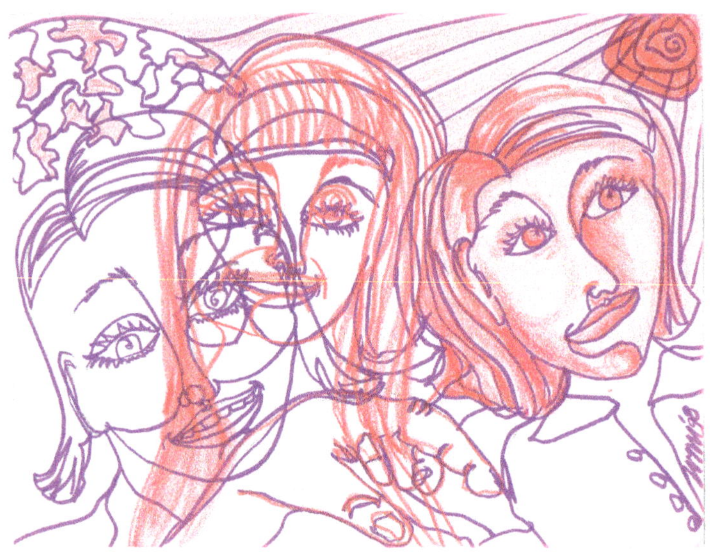

It's All Coming Together

In many ways, involving Heide in my reflective artmaking process forced me to deal with the issue of time. This benefit was not without a downside—namely the pressure that both Heide and I felt to produce art pieces. Knowing we were under a time line, we had to reflect through artmaking whether we had the desire or inspiration to do so. As Heide revealed in her log:

> *I couldn't reflect. I tried several times, but I couldn't think of anything to reflect on. That alone made me very frustrated.*

In another entry titled "It's all coming together," Heide mentioned her fear of letting me down, especially she said, because I have so much at stake (meaning my dissertation).

I recall times when I wanted to sleep or watch television, but would think of Heide working in her sketchbook and feel compelled to do the same. Both Heide and I experienced times when we were unable to create anything and during our last conference we reminisced about the guilt we felt:

> *Heide: I'd think, "Well Wendy is at home reflecting, why can't I?" I felt horrible on those days. I also noticed that the days I couldn't reflect were the days I was doing the planning, a lot more of the nitty-gritty part of this job; not the more fun, creative side of it.*

> *Wendy: I had trouble reflecting on the days that ran more smoothly. When there weren't any highs or lows—just a regular day—nothing triggered any thoughts. There were also a lot of outside things that I reflected on, like inclusion, praise, the schedule. It wasn't so much the stuff that happened during the day in a particular class. I think part of that was because you were teaching, and I wasn't. I would go home feeling so rotten that you were drawing away, and I wasn't. And I was the one who asked you to do this project in the first place.*

Some of the most difficult times we had making pieces in our sketchbooks occurred during the initial week, possibly due to the ambiguous nature of the project. During this time, we created images without seeing each other's work. Both of us were unsure if what we were doing was "correct." The uncertainty dissipated once we began sharing our sketchbooks and discussing the ideas surrounding the images. This, in turn, allowed us to feel freer to experiment with our ideas, media, and abstractions.

My mind was also put at ease after seeing Heide's work. Her use of media, especially the construction paper entries, and the two-page layouts stretched my imagination and encouraged me to try new ways to create reflective images. The expectation for sharing forced me to create each night. Without Heide, I became more haphazard about drawing, thinking no one would notice. I was mistaken. Someone else did notice:

> *A tall, slim fifth grade girl quietly came up to me at*
> *the end of class and asked if I had any more drawings*
> *in my sketchbook. I think I actually turned red with*
> *embarrassment when I told her, "No, I don't have any*
> *new drawings." My embarrassment grew when she*
> *said she had completely filled her sketchbook and was*
> *asking for a new one for Christmas.*

I suppose peer pressure can be exerted from many sources, even much younger ones who seem to ask the right questions at the right time.

With the freedom to create, however, came the pain and the frustration that can accompany the reflective artmaking process. Prior to the inquiry, I considered myself to be an excellent art teacher. Adding the role of art-researcher began to reveal previously unrecognized sides of myself—sides, quite frankly, I did not want to see. As Posner[1] points out, reflection assists teachers in improving their practices, but it does not necessarily come without consequences. Ditchburn, Jardine and Prasow describe two stages of reflection. One is "stepping back" from a situation to "see it anew."[2] Here the teacher becomes a detached observer of his or her actions.

During the first week of my project, there was a freshness to the experience and an excitement about learning new things about my pedagogy. Soon, however, I was shocked to see actions like the hands-down gesture which might have a negative effect on the children. Ditchburn et al. refer to this second step of reflection as "being taken aback":

> Often this is a disorienting experience which forces
> us to reconsider what we are doing, what we have
> assumed. It is a powerful experience, since it occasions
> a breakdown of the prejudice of our experience of the

---

1   George J. Posner, *Field Experience: A Guide to Reflective Teaching.* 3rd ed. (New York: Longman, 1993).

2   Susan Ditchburn, David Jardine, and Cynthia Prasow, "The Emerging Voice: Toward Reflective Practice," *Teaching and Learning* 4, no.2 (1990): 21.

world, often accompanied by feelings of accusation and culpability. [3]

As I progressed through the reflective artmaking process and began to see the potentially negative effects of my teaching, I was beginning to experience feelings of self-accusation and accountability. Admitting my embarrassing and painful self-discoveries to Heide added to a spiraling negativity. Stepping into the self-observer role led to feeling that everything I did was wrong, reaching a point when I considered quitting my job. Finally, I wrote the following journal entry:

> *If someone read most of my reflections they'd probably think I was a terrible teacher, but I'm not that bad. I need to get back to what I do right instead of everything I do wrong. If I focus only on the bad things, I may end up frustrated or disgusted with myself and as a result do nothing, think it's hopeless, or leave my job. I've always said if I got burnt out I would quit right then and there so I don't hurt the kids.*

The next day, I tried to notice ways in which I taught well or responded positively to the children. What resulted was the sketch, "Balancing Things Out," in which I emphasize the need to balance the positive and negative views of my teaching. The negativism re-emerged on occasion, but soon after, I started examining issues that were neither positive nor negative. They were simply interesting, such as trying new approaches to a particular unit, rearranging my classroom, or finding time to listen to students. My points of interest were more wide-open and offered the potential for curiosity, exploration, discovery, surprise, and growth—all of which seemed more generative, creative, and meaningful than simplistic positive or negative judgments. Entering into exploration of these issues helped me to alter my teaching behaviors. Smith says if teachers can get past the "taken aback" feelings that arise during self-examination, reflection can increase awareness of

---

3   Ditchburn, Jardine, and Prasow, 21

the contradictions between what individuals say they do and what they actually do.[4] Living with the contradictions creates the potential for new learning. As Briscoe points out:

> Individual commitment to change on the part of a teacher is not sufficient to induce the desired changes. It is apparent that if changes are to occur in practice teachers must examine their beliefs, judgments, and thoughts regarding what they do and how they do it. Teachers need time to reflect on their own practices, assign language to their actions, and construct new knowledge which is consistent with the role metaphors they use to make sense of changes in their practice. [5]

Becoming aware of who I was as an art teacher, what my teaching practices were, and what I wanted them to become persuaded me to enact changes in my pedagogy. I have come to realize that change does not occur immediately, nor will I become a perfect teacher. But I have gained a process through which I can continue to grow.

The shock of seeing my less desirable teaching practices was accompanied by the shock of seeing myself as a poor artist. Attempts to visually reconstruct my teaching experiences did not match the stunning images I saw in my head. I resonate with Bayles and Orland who say

> ...making art is chancy...Uncertainty is the essential, inevitable, and all-pervasive companion to your desire to make art. And tolerance for uncertainty is the prerequisite to succeeding.[6]

I sometimes see my students hesitate, erase or cover their drawings when others peer over their shoulders. I have wondered why this is so. "It's not a big deal, just draw," I tell them. Putting my own pencil to paper, I empathized with their hesitation, their pause. Making art is

---

4   Smith, 76.
5   Carole Briscoe, "Beliefs, Metaphors and Teacher Change: A Case Study," Paper presented at the Annual Meeting of the American Educational Association, Boston, MA, April 1990, 16.
6   Bayles and Orland, 21.

chancy. Trying to bring forth an image and not being able to do so, made me feel inferior, angry with myself, and embarrassed to have others see my lack of progress. Every time we make the decision to create we take a chance. As a student, I protected myself from the "chancy-ness" by making art that would not be as painful or as personal. I painted landscapes for people's walls by copying from photographs, painted cartoonish sweatshirts for gifts, and dutifully did what my art teachers told me to do. I didn't experience the pleasure of creating for myself or the depth of passion which erupted when I started bringing my internal pictures to life. That passion was riddled with fear, a fear so great that many times I was tempted to quit. But the process could also be soothing, calming, relaxing—meeting a need I did not know I had. In the end, this calming side of artmaking outweighs the difficult side, causing me to crave time for drawing in my sketchbook.

PORTFOLIO ARTIFACT #21

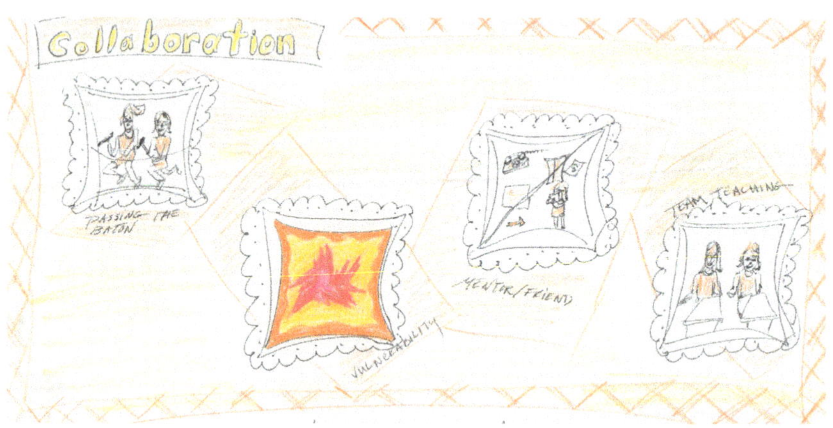

Working Together

nitially I chose to collaborate with Heide because I thought it might save some time. Later I discovered art education discourses calling for cooperating teachers to engage their student teachers in some form of reflection. Klein[1] says one way to develop leadership in pre-service teachers is to provide a tool by which they can assess and reflect upon their own student teaching experiences. Carole Henry[2] echoes this view, saying if we want student art teachers to be reflective practicing teachers, then we must prepare them with ways to reflect and opportunities to do so. She also suggests that through reflection, student art teachers are better able to see themselves change from students into teachers, recognizing their progress while realizing they still need to grow. Although my initial collaboration with Heide seemed to be one of convenience, we discovered a collaborative effort had positive effects on both of us, individually and in our relationship.

1　Sheri Klein, "Teacher/leaders: Developing Leadership in Pre-service Art Teachers," *National Art Education Association Advisory* (Summer 1998).

2　Carole Henry, "The Role of Reflection in Student Teachers' Perceptions of Their Professional Development," *Art Education* 53, no. 2 (1999).

Heide noted that our relationship changed quickly from one of teacher and student to colleagues. According to Henry, student art teachers expressed concerns about their relationships with their cooperating teachers including being in proximity to another person all day and establishing their own professional space. Seeing and hearing about my insecurities let Heide relate to me as a peer, someone she could talk with freely, dispelling some of the concerns raised by Henry. In one journal entry, Heide wrote:

> *It really is a fine line [between friend and mentor], one that must be maintained professionally. However, I'm starting to realize how a lot of our experiences happen on both sides, or happen because one side affects the other. The whole idea of us reflecting together and sharing such personal experiences really shows how comfortable we are with one another. Often people have said to me, "You share these ideas and thoughts with Wendy?" It is the experience of sharing that enables me to give my teaching my all in front of her... Once I got to know my cooperating teacher, I saw that it's okay to be friends. There's a fine line between the two realms, and Wendy and I have prospered from crossing that line when necessary.*

Collaborating about lesson ideas, making art together, and teaching together combined with the goal of discovering the nature of reflective artmaking cemented our relationship and helped us grow as teachers. As Beck[3] points out, reflection done collaboratively has a greater potential to motivate change in practice or ideology.

I was intrigued by the collaborative nature of this project since, as an only child, I tended to do things alone. Heide, also an only child, mentioned how much she enjoys her private time. During most of my teaching experience, I had kept to myself. Though I felt lonely at times, rarely did I seek out other teachers with whom to work or reflect.

Collaborating with someone who was visually literate deepened our conference conversations. While viewing the visual images, there

---

3 Beck, *Teacher Reflective Practice.*

was a mutual, tacit understanding about each other's pieces. The images themselves told a story which we were able to read, providing us with insights into their meanings that needed no verbal enhancement. In an article titled, "Quiltmaking as Metaphor," Wendy Stephenson described watching her grandmother draw a crayon landscape of their home. Although she was only seven, she recalled being mesmerized as she watched her grandmother select purple for the tip of a mountain and the shadows. She wrote:

> I thought yes, purple. I've seen it that way in the snow…a kind of apricot purple. I'd seen it that way looking up at the mountain from the kitchen window while eating breakfast. Her picture made me realize what I saw.[4]

Now older, working as an artist herself, Stephenson says she attempts to help others see beauty as her grandmother helped her see the color of the mountain. This story reflects the ways in which Heide's and my artwork helped me to see anew what was occurring in my teaching practice. Elizabeth Vallance reminds me that "aesthetic responses at their most natural are spontaneous, unplanned, usually enjoyable, and they invariably offer us an unexpected new perspective on something we already know."[5] This was certainly true for me as I sketched the events of my pedagogical practice.

---

4 Irwin, Rita L., Wendy Stephenson, Helen Robertson, Aileen Neale, Rosa Mastri, and Nancy Crawford. "Quiltmaking Metaphor: Creating a Feminist Political Consciousness for Art Pedagogues," In *Women Art Educators IV: Herstories, Ourstories, Future Stories*, edited by Elizabeth J. Sacca and Enid Zimmerman, 100-111. Boucherville, Quebec: Canadian Society for Education through Art. 1998.

5 Elizabeth Vallance, "Aesthetic Inquiry: Art Criticism," in *Forms of Curriculum Inquiry*, ed. Edmund Short (Albany NY: State University of New York, 1991), 159.

PORTFOLIO ARTIFACT #22

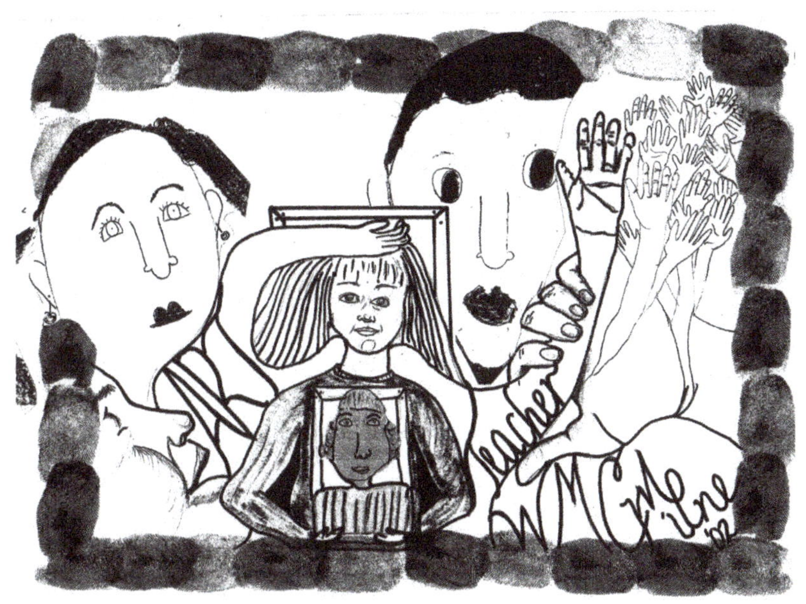

Aesthetic Knowing

An aspect of reflective artmaking which continues to surprise me is its quality of visual memory—moments when pictures or images enter my mind. I can see them quite clearly as if they are actually in front of me. Words, even ones I wrote just a few months earlier, are easily forgotten, whereas images viewed long ago are recalled instantly. For example, whenever I find myself about to make the "hands down" gesture, I instantly see the sketch I drew. Seeing these visually stored memories have been helpful in breaking habits I no longer value.

Carole Henry recommends student art teachers use writing as a means of reflection because writing provides time to process thoughts at a slower pace. She cites a variety of authors who also suggest that writing enhances reflection. While writing has been important to my process, making, viewing, and critiquing art slowed my thinking and allowed me to look more carefully at pedagogical events. Retired art teacher/artist Jo Leeds commented in an interview with Julia Kellman that she became interested in art at an early age and wondered why "one should write words when one could make images of things instead."[1] *The Visual Arts Education Reform Handbook* advocates "…art is a mode of inquiry and expression that helps people communicate ideas that could not be captured in words alone." [2] Grauer and Sandell[3] use visual journals with K-12 pre-service and practicing teachers to promote reflection. Such calls for visual reflection point to the importance of aesthetic ways of knowing.[4]

---

1   Leeds, 44.
2   National Art Education Association, *Visual Arts Education Reform Handbook*, 8.
3   Kit Grauer, and Renee Sandell , The Visual Journal and Teacher Development," Paper presented at the Annual Meeting of the National Art Education Association, Washington, D.C., 1999.
4   The concept of visual journaling has become prevalent in recent years. See for example, Hadar, 2019; Institute for Arts Integration and STEAM; redesign, 2020. Full citations in Bibliography.

Reflective Highlights:
Gathering Together Threads of Thought

During high school and college there was little substance in my art works. Rarely, if ever, did I reflect on the artmaking process or the final product. Although the idea of reflecting on art emerged during my college years, I did not fully comprehend why I felt it was important to have my students reflect. Thus, I gave them many opportunities to think and write about their processes and products, but was unable to clearly explain why I did so. Researchers like Smith[5] and Delacruz[6] say that many master teachers often have difficulty explaining what it is that they do and what strategies they use. Brubacher, Case and Reagan[7] suggest many teachers rely on intuition during their daily teaching. Unlike reflection, intuition does not oblige teachers to consider what has been done, why it has been done, and what changes need to occur. Posner advocates incorporating reflection into educational practice because

> …non-reflective teachers rely on routine behavior and are guided more by impulse, tradition, and authority than by reflection. They simplify their professional lives by uncritically accepting everyday reality in schools. In contrast, reflective teachers actively, persistently, and carefully consider and reconsider beliefs and practice in light of the grounds that support them and the further consequences to which they lead.[8]

Reid supports the important relationship of intuition and reflection, saying both can enhance understanding, especially in the arts. Interpreting Kant's ideas about aesthetic intuition, Reid explains:

---

5   Smith, "Qualitative Focus Group."
6   Delacruz, *Design for Inquiry.*
7   John W. Brubacher, Charles W. Case, and Timothy G. Reagan, *Becoming a Reflective Educator: How to Build a Culture of Inquiry in the Schools.* (Thousand Oaks, CA: Corwin Press, 1994).
8   Posner, *Field Experience.*

> ...art without reflection and study can be half-blind,
> and that reflective thinking, without a return to
> aesthetic intuition, is empty. What is needed is the
> absorption of discursively reflective thinking and
> study and assimilation of it, a conscious forgetting of
> it, and a return illuminated enriched intuition.[9]

I used a combination of intuition and forms of reflection while moving through my inquiry. Often I said to myself, "This just feels right." I proceeded with the inquiry and teaching, not knowing what would come. Reflecting on these intuitive moments helped me examine exactly what was occurring during the inquiry and why the process was (or was not) important to my pedagogical understanding. This reflective period led to what Reid called "illuminated enriched intuition."

Although I was surrounded by art during my years of teaching, I quit making art and focused on oral and written forms of explanation. Regardless of environment—my elementary classroom, college art courses I took and taught, and art education workshops—I tended to write or talk. I missed seeing the relevance of doing art myself, although I espoused the views of Gardner's[10] spatial intelligences and claimed to be visually literate.

When I finally came to the concept of reflective artmaking and engaged in the process, I began to realize that I come to know aesthetically. For me, this encompasses making, viewing, and critiquing art. Reid contends that aesthetic knowing involves functioning as a whole, whereas scientific knowing relies mostly upon using our "heads."[11]

Many aspects of reflective artmaking (i.e., sketching, reviewing sketches to discern patterns, creating *Portfolio Artifacts*) revolve around a full range of feelings, including pain, pressure, frustration, joy and desire. Heyfron tells us that in producing art, the maker transforms her feelings into tangible objects, thus showing that her feelings exist.

---

9   Reid, "Aesthetic Knowledge in the Art," 39-40.

10 Howard Gardner, "Multiple Intelligences: Implications for Art and Creativity," in *Artistic Intelligences: Implications for Education*, ed. William J. Moody (New York: Teachers College Press, 1990).

11 Recently, my thinking about this relationship has been challenged by the writing of Shawn Otto who contends that science in its most profound form is intuitive and aesthetic.

He further writes, "feeling is a distinctive way of recognizing the significance of human existence, a kind of knowing with self, and we gain insight into this significance of how things are through engaging in art." Heyfron contends, "The knowledge we gain in art is immediate and direct. The art object provides the structure by which both artist and his public are able to experience, and thus, intuitively know otherwise inchoate and ineffable feelings." [12]

And, as Reid argues, feelings are:

> ...intrinsic to knowledge and understanding of the arts...Feeling is immediate awareness of the whole content of one's conscious experience, an indwelling in it...Feeling also shares in the transitiveness or outward-directedness of cognition towards its objects, so that feeling can be properly called "cognitive." [13]

Further, he says aesthetic knowing involves the interaction of the mind and the body, and of "thinking, imagining, acting and feeling." [14] Susanne Langer states that "art is the creation of forms symbolic of human feeling." [15]

Others remind us the arts provide unique ways of knowing about the world and should be considered central to learning. [16] "The Arts Education Partnership Working Group" takes the position that the arts are forms of understanding and ways of knowing that are valuable in and of themselves. [17]

Although I am capable of communicating and learning verbally, I understand better when I create artistically. The creative act of visually reconstructing an event or concept yields deeper understandings

---

12 Victor Heyfron, "The Objective Status of Aesthetic Knowing," in *The Arts: A Way of Knowing*, ed. M. Ross (New York: Pergamon Press, 1983) 46, 71, .

13 Reid, 22-23.

14 Reid, 25.

15 Susanne K. Langer, *Feeling and Form* (London: Routledge, 1953), 32.

16 *Coming to Our Senses: The Significance of the Arts for American Education*. Panel Report from the American Council for the Arts. New York, NY: 1977.

17 James D. Wolfensohn, and Harrold M. Williams, *The Power of the Arts to Transform Education: An Agenda for Action*. John F. Kennedy Center for the Performing Arts, Washington D.C., J. Paul Getty Trust, Santa Monica, CA. 1993.

in which I am able to make unanticipated connections to create a new whole. As Jongeward[18] indicates, a "new whole" can then be communicated verbally to others who may be less visually inclined.

Cohen and Gainer[19] suggest that verbal explanations may not be needed in an artistic arena, because art can function as a language that makes ideas clearer and inspires more ideas. Indeed, Parsons contends "there is no real need to use language when we think artistically or aesthetically."[20] However, in the educational realm, all verbal communication cannot be abandoned. In an educational research setting, it is the researcher's responsibility to communicate her processes, products, and insights to a variety of audiences where verbal communication predominates. Simply supplying the reader with visuals is less likely to contribute in a meaningful way to educational discourses. Teacher educator and narrative inquirer, Patricia L. McMahon[21] suggests that an integral part of arts-based research is a verbal "interrogation" of the work of art. I choose to use both words and visuals, because I wish to speak to art *education* communities. Parsons adds that words are not necessary when thinking in art but when viewing an abstract art object we "need to talk about artworks as well as look at them because we need to connect them with aspects of both the art world and the world in general." He continues:

> On the interpretive view, then, language becomes an essential part of the cognition in the art. If an object is unclear, we try to express our sense of it in words. In practice, this means we must try to say it as well as see it. More accurately, since only part of the sense will be more clear in the interpretation than in the object itself, and vice versa, we must be able to discuss what is hard to see and to see what is hard to say. And then the two kinds of thinking—that is thinking in two different

---

18 Jongeward, "Visual Portraits."
19 Cohen and Gainer, *Art, Another Language for Learning.*
20 Michael J. Parsons, "Cognition as Interpretation in Art Education," in *The Arts, Education and Aesthetic Knowing: Ninety-first Yearbook of the National Society for the Study of Education* (Chicago, Chicago Press, 1992), 79.
21 See McMahon 1993, 2000, and 2018. See full citations in Bibliography.

media—will be interactive and combine to form one understanding. We clarify in words relations of the object so we can see those relations in the object. It follows that the words are not just a crutch. They are as important as the looking. Not more important but equally so, because both the talking and the looking are constitutive of the artwork, of the qualities it has and the meanings it carries. If we stayed with thinking in one medium, interpretation would be impossible and the object would remain obscure.[22]

In conducting a study of reflective artmaking, I had to weave together words and images in the hope of reaching as wide an audience as possible. To write the words more easily, I needed to first express my ideas visually. The visuals, in turn, helped me to focus on what needed to be written. Through this I aimed to provide others with a vicarious experience of reflective artmaking, for, as Elliot Eisner tells us, "…art informs us about things that we didn't have the opportunity to experience directly."[23]

---

22 Parsons, "Cognition and Interpretation," 82.
23 Elliot W. Eisner, "Implications of Artistic Intelligences for Education," in *Artistic Intelligences*, ed. William J. Moody (New York: Teachers College Press, 1990), 34.

Portfolio Theme

REFLECTIVE ARTMAKING IN PERSPECTIVE

A Time of Transition

As I mentioned previously, the catalyst for immersing myself in reflective artmaking was the academic requirement to complete a doctoral dissertation. Once I completed this academic task, however, I continued this process of professional learning. In all honesty, I was not as diligent in sketching as I had been during the intensive year of my inquiry. Nevertheless, I continued to value the process of artmaking and drew upon it as a source of comfort during several stressful years. I also embraced it as a way to connect in a personally meaningful way with state requirements for documenting my teaching expertise. The Portfolio Artifacts under this theme offer examples of how I incorporated reflective artmaking into my on-going professional life.

PORTFOLIO ARTIFACT #23

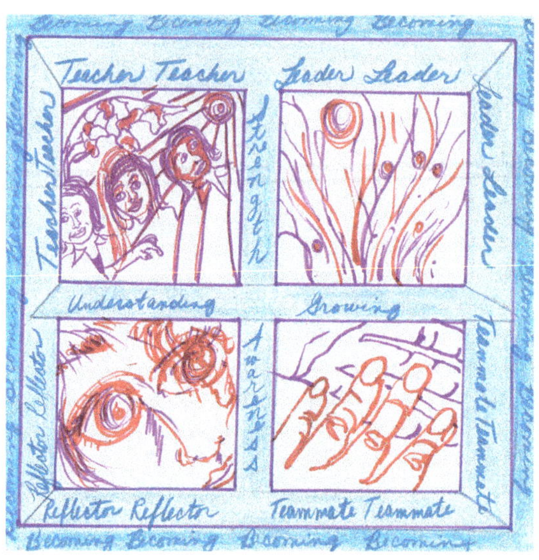

From Dissertation Study to Professional Learning

During the years after defending my dissertation, I immersed myself in reading "fun" books and returned to running. Once again, I lost touch with my artmaking and worked only sporadically in my sketchbooks. As time went on, however, I was drawn back to reflective artmaking for personal and professional growth.

PORTFOLIO ARTIFACT #24

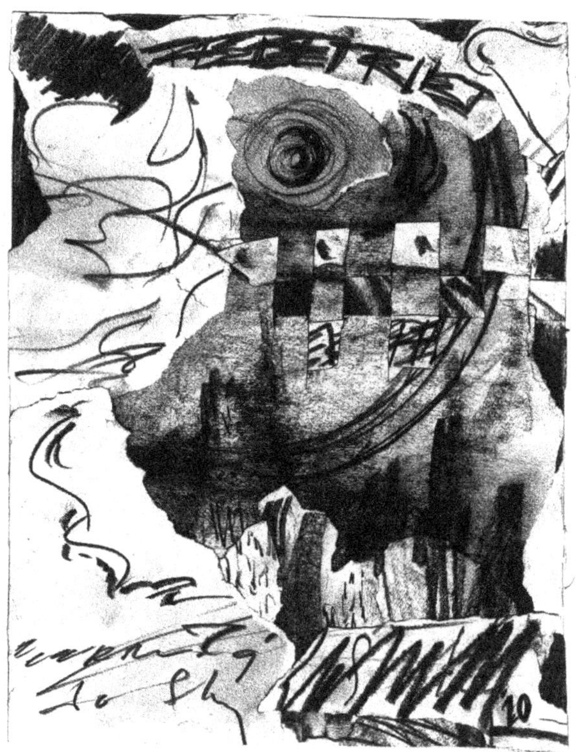

Grief

In 2010 I experienced a painful loss in my family and turned to artmaking once again. The artmaking during this long period of grief was more of a distraction for me rather than an examination of my grief or a way to move past it. In only one instance did I dip into those waters of grief through artmaking. The heavily charcoaled lines swirling and weaving together depict my innermost thoughts. I found it too painful to continue in this manner and moved back to working on my watercolor technique rather than personal understanding.

PORTFOLIO ARTIFACT #25

Differentiated Project 2014

In this year, my school district adopted the state's requirement that teachers document their growth through a Differentiated Portfolio. I pushed hard for the district to accept a visual portfolio as an acceptable format for documentation. Thus, once again, I could use my sketchbook to reflect on my practice. During this year, I used Danielson's framework to incorporate as much information as I could into the portfolio in an effort to demonstrate as thoroughly as possible my professional competence and accomplishments. I must confess that the images in this portfolio were more for artistic embellishment than expressions of reflective insights.

PORTFOLIO ARTIFACT #26

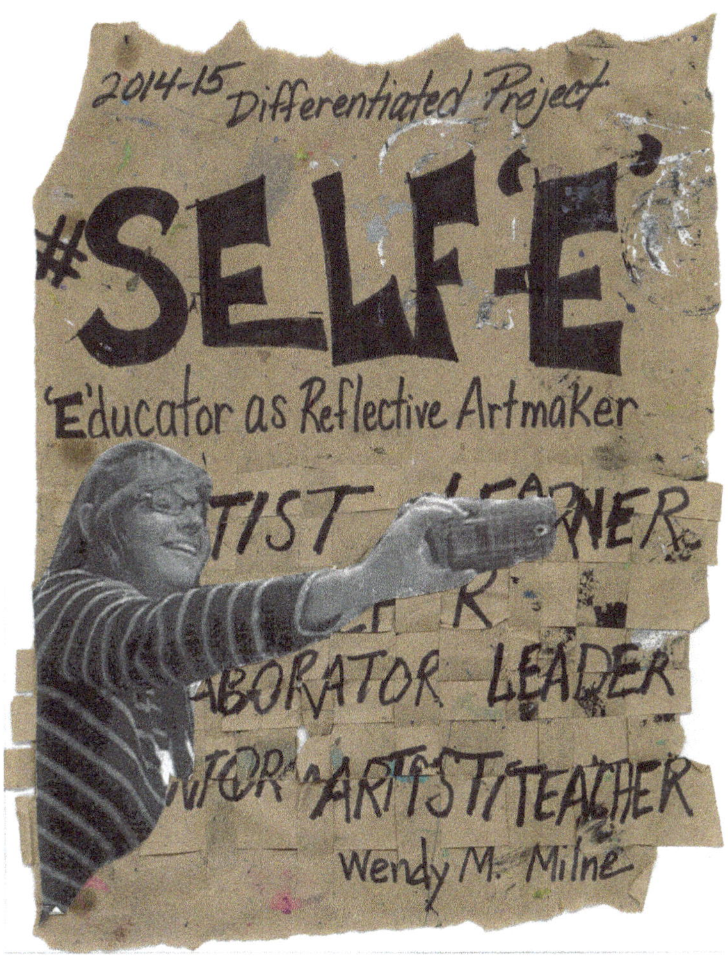

Differentiated Project 2015

During this year, I was determined to meet my needs as a teacher rather than draw what I thought the administration would want. Thus, I returned to reflective artmaking as I understood it to be . Re-immersing myself in this form of reflection proved incredibly rewarding.

PORTFOLIO ARTIFACT #27

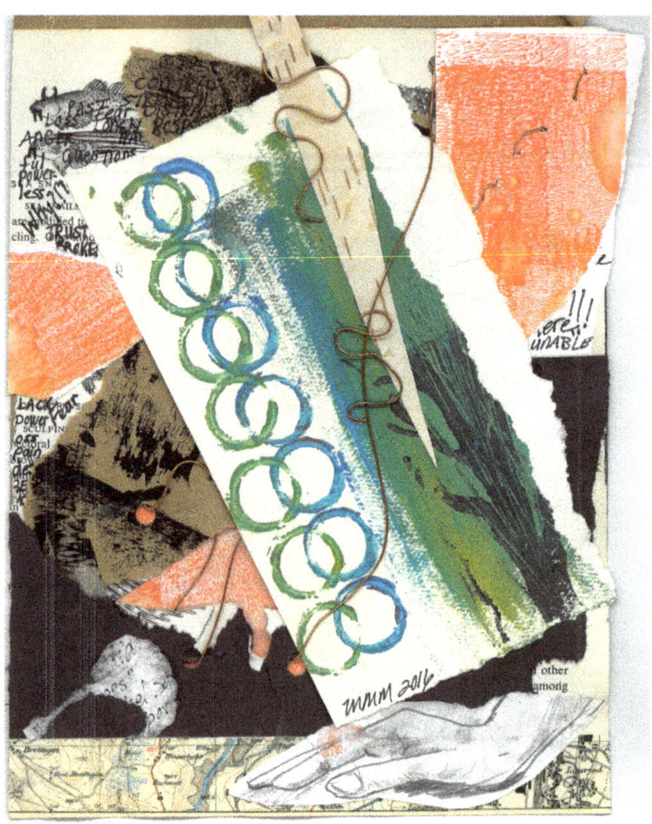

Differentiated Project 2016

The next school year came with turbulence and sadness in our school. Unlike in 2010 when I could not explore my grief through my art, I invested fully in the artmaking process and used my sketchbook as a cathartic means of surviving the school year. The entire sketchbook was filled with painful, abstract images and words as illustrated by this image.

REFLECTIVE ARTMAKING
IN PERSPECTIVE

Looking Forward

I continue using my sketchbook in various formats to suit my needs and that of the state. I have continued to raise the possibility of collaborative reflective artmaking with several student teachers. Sadly, none of them expressed a strong desire to engage in the process, and I did not push them to do so. I think back to Heide's openness to joining me in our exploration and see again, how special that relationship was and how lucky I was to have her be part of it.

I began to work on this book in 2020 just as the COVID-19 pandemic swept across the United States, disrupting the familiar structures and routines of schooling. Like teachers throughout the country, I was challenged to respond in new and unimagined ways to fulfill my responsibilities to students. When predictions that the pandemic would be relatively short-lived proved to be inaccurate, I faced the 2020-2021 school year with considerable uncertainty. I could not count on a "new normal" as my district moved to a hybrid model of in person and cyber classes. Shortly into the year, several buildings closed and shifted entirely to distance teaching-learning. At any time, my building could be next. Accepting an invitation to post my thoughts on a website designed to support scholar-practitioners, I created the image below.[1]

---

1   Visit the scholarpractitionernexus.com if you would like to share your experiences as an educator. The discussion threads continue to evolve, based on the concerns of engaged in any level of teaching-learning.

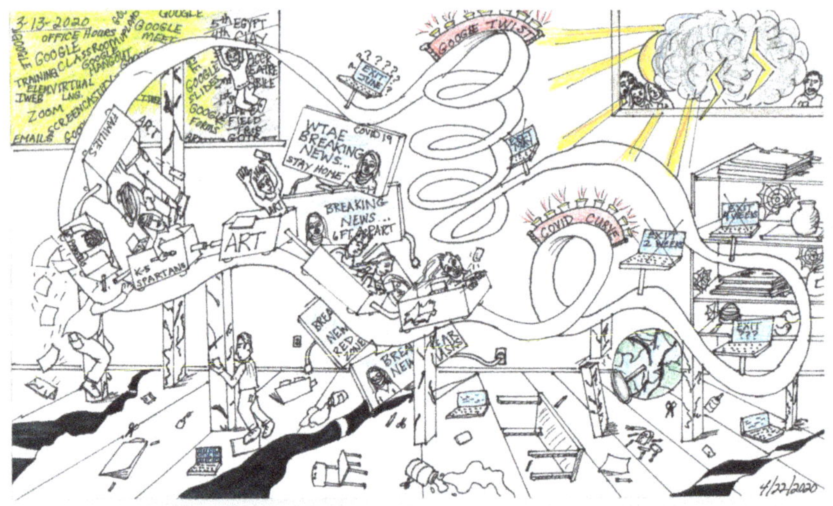

As I ponder this "new normal," I realize that neither I nor anyone else can predict the lasting effects caused by the stresses of the pandemic. Just as I came to understand that an excessive need to control my classroom might undermine the very learning I hoped to foster, I now recognize the limited control I have over the broader context of my professional life. I, like so many other teachers, stand at a crossroads. I can succumb to the stresses of a world beyond my control, or I can find ways to manage the stress and continue to strive for a personally and professionally meaningful life. I trust that the lessons I have learned about reflective artmaking will sustain me as I choose to move forward with hope that life will return, not to what it was, but to something new and exciting. Re-viewing the *Portfolio Artifacts* and the thoughts they represent reminds me that, as always, my relationships with students lie at the heart of my practice.

Although my particular process of reflective artmaking may not fit with everyone's style of professional learning, I hope that the artifacts I have shared will give others ideas for meeting whatever challenges we face in the coming years.

Bibliography

Adams, Henry. *The Education of Henry Adams*. Boston: Houghton Mifflin, 1918/1973.

Anglin, Jacqueline M. "Developing a Creative Relationship with Your Art Student Teacher." *Art Education* 44, no. 2 (1991): 47-53.

Anderson, Rae. "A Case Study of the Artist as Teacher through the Video Work of Martha Davis." *Studies in Art Education* 39, no. 1 (1997): 37-56.

Aukerman, Ruth. "Childrens' Art from Fine Art: An Exemplar Approach to Teaching Elementary Children." *School Arts* (April 1992): 30-32.

Bayles, David and Ted Orland. *Art and Fear: Observations on the Perils (and Rewards) of Artmaking*. Santa Barbara, CA: Capra Press, 1993.

Beck, Linda. *Teacher Reflective Practice: Documenting Reflection in a Teacher Collaborative Group*. Unpublished doctoral thesis, University of California, 1997.

Black, Susan. "Art and Soul." *The Executive Educator* 18, no. 1 (January 1996): 19-21.

Bolanos, Patricia. "Agents of Change: Artists and Teachers." *Art Education* 39, no. 6 (1986): 49-52.

Bolin, Paul E. "Reflection." *Art Education* 52, no. 2 (1999): 4-5.

Briscoe, Carole. "Beliefs, Metaphors and Teacher Change: A Case Study." Paper presented at the Annual Meeting of the American Educational Association, Boston, MA, April 1990.

Burnard, Pamela, and Sarah Hennessy, eds. *Reflective Practices in Arts Education*. New York: Springer-Verlag, 2006.

Brubacher, John W., Charles W. Case, and Timothy G. Reagan. *Becoming a Reflective Educator: How to Build a Culture of Inquiry in the Schools*. Thousand Oaks, CA: Corwin, 1994.

Caldwell, Barbara. "An Enduring Coterie of Soul Friends: Photographs of Authentic Teaching." In *Women Art Educators V: Conversations Across Time*, edited by Kit Grauer, Rita L. Irwin and Enid Zimmerman, 228-236. Reston, VA: NAEA National Art Education Association. 2003.

Cohen, Elaine P., and Ruth S. Gainer. *Art, Another Language for Learning*. New York: Schocken Books, 1971.

Coming to Our Senses: The Significance of the Arts for American Education. Panel Report from the American Council for the Arts. New York, NY: 1977.

Conant, Howard. "Season of Decline." In *New Ideas in Art Education: A Critical Anthology*, edited by Gregory Battcock. New York: Dutton, 1973.

Csikszentmihalyi, Mihaly. *Flow: The Psychology of Optimal Experience*. New York: Harper & Row, 1990.

Cuban, Larry. "Persistent Instruction: Another Look at Constancy in the Classroom." *Phi Delta Kapan* 68, no. 1 (1986): 7-11.

Day, Michael. "Art Education for the New Millennium." Keynote speech presented at the Annual Convention of the National Art Education Association, Chicago, IL, April 1998.

Delacruz, Elizabeth M. *Design for Inquiry: Instructional Theory, Research and Practice in Art Education.* Reston, VA: National Art Education Association, 1997.

Dewey, John. *How We Think: A Restatement of the Relation of Reflective Thinking to the Educative Process.* Boston: Houghton Mifflin. 1933/1998

Dewey, John. *Art as Experience.* New York: First Perigree Printing, 1934/1980.

Ditchburn, Susan, David Jardine, and Cynthia Prasow. "The Emerging Voice: Toward Reflective Practice." *Teaching and Learning* 4, no. 2 (1990): 20-29.

Dobbs, Stephen M. *Learning in and through Art.* CA: The Getty Education Institute for the Arts, 1998.

Douglas, Katherine M., and Diane B. Jaquithm eds. *Choice-Based Art Education in the Classroom (TAB).* New York: Teachers College Press, 2018.

Efland, Arthur, Kerry Freedman, and Patricia Stuhr. *Postmodern Art Education: An Approach to Curriculum.* Reston, VA, The National Art Education Association, 1996.

Eisner, Elliot W. "Aesthetic Modes of Knowing." In *Learning and Teaching the Ways of Knowing: Eighty-fourth Yearbook of the National Society for the Study of Education*, edited by Elliot W. Eisner, 23-36. Chicago: University of Chicago Press, 1985.

Eisner, Elliot W. *Educating Artistic Vision.* Reston, VA: The National Art Education Association, 1997.

Eisner, Elliot W. *The Enlightened Eye: Qualitative Inquiry and the Enhancement of Educational Practice.* New York: MacMillan, 1991.

Eisner, Elliot W. "Implications of Artistic Intelligences for Education." In *Artistic Intelligences*, edited by William J. Moody, 31-42. New York: Teachers College Press, 1990.

Eisner, Elliot W. "Structure and Magic in Discipline-based Art Education." In *Critical Studies in Art and Design Education*, edited by David Thistlewood, 14-25. Portsmouth, NH: Heinemann, 1991.

Erickson, Mary, and Katter, Eldon. "Integrating the Four Components of a Quality Art Education." *National Arts Education Association Advisory.* Alexandria, VA: National Arts Education Association, Fall 1988.

Ernst, Karen. *Picturing Learning: Artists and Writers in the Classroom.* Portsmouth, MA: Heinemann, 1994.

Feldman, Edmund B. "Best Advice and Counsel to Art Teachers." *Art Education* 46, no.5 (1993): 58-59.

Feldman, Edmond B. "Clay: Arguments for and with. Proceedings of the Symposium: The Case for Clay in Art Education." *Studio Potter* 16, no. 2 (1988): 18-23.

Galbraith, Lynn. *Merging the Research on Teaching with Art Content: A Qualitative Study of a Preservice Art Education Course for General Elementary Teachers.* Unpublished doctoral dissertation. University of Nebraska, 1988.

Galbraith, Lynn. "Research-oriented Art Teachers: Implications for Art Teaching." *Art Education* 41, no. 5 (1988): 50-53.

Gardner, Howard. "Multiple Intelligences: Implications for Art and Creativity." In *Artistic Intelligences: Implications for Education*, edited by William J. Moody, 11-30. New York: Teachers College Press, 1990.

Garman, Noreen B., and Maria Piantanida, eds. *The Authority to Imagine: The Struggle toward Representation in Dissertation Writing.* Pittsburgh: Learning Moments Press, 2018.

Grauer, Kit, and Renee Sandell. "The Visual Journal and Teacher Development." Paper presented at the Annual Meeting of the National Art Education Association. Washington, DC. 1999.

Hadar, Rakefet. *Layers of Meaning—Elements of Visual Journaling.* Translated by Dalit Shmueli. 2019.

Henry Carole. "The Role of Reflection in Student Teachers' Perceptions of Their Professional Development." *Art Education* 52, no.2 (1999): 14-20.

Heyfron, Victor. "The Objective Status of Aesthetic Knowing." In *The Arts: A Way of Knowing*, edited by M Ross, 43-72. New York: Pergamon Press, 1983.

Institute for Arts Integration and STEAM. Essential Tips for Visual Journaling. Retrieved December 27, 2020 from https://artsintegration.com/2019/03/01/essential-tips-for-visual-journaling/

Irwin, Rita L., Wendy Stephenson, Helen Robertson, Aileen Neale, Rosa Mastri, and Nancy Crawford. "Quiltmaking Metaphor: Creating a Feminist Political Consciousness for Art Pedagogues." In *Women Art Educators IV: Herstories, Ourstories, Future Stories*, edited by Elizabeth J. Sacca and Enid Zimmerman, 100-111. Boucherville, Quebec: Canadian Society for Education through Art. 1998.

Irwin, Rita L. "Listening to the Shapes of Collaborative Artmaking." *Art Education* 52, no. 2 (1999): 35-39.

Jackson, Phillip W. *Life in Classrooms.* New York: Holt, Rinehart and Winston, 1968.

Jeffers, Carol S. "Child-centered and Discipline-based Art Education: Metaphor and Meaning." *Art Education* 43, no. 2 (1990): 16-21.

Jongeward, Carolyn. "Visual Portraits: An Artistic Approach to Qualitative Educational Research." Paper presented at the Annual Meeting of the American Educational Research Association, Chicago, IL, April 1997.

Kaufman, Irving. "The Subject is Art." *Studies in Art Education* 30, no. 2 (1989): 84-92.

Kliebard, Herbert M. "A Perspective on Twentieth-century Curriculum Reforms." *In Learning and Teaching the Ways of Knowing: Eighty-fourth Yearbook of the National Society for the Study of Education*, edited by Elliot W. Eisner, 1-22. Chicago: The University of Chicago Press, 1985.

Klein, Sheri. "Teacher/leaders: Developing Leadership in Pre-service Art Teachers." *National Art Education Association Advisory*. Alexandria, VA: National Arts Education Association Summer 1998.

Langer, Susanne K. *Feeling and Form*. London: Routledge, 1953.

Leeds, Jo. An interview by Julia Kellman. "The Voice of an Elder. Jo Leeds, Artist Teacher, A Personal Perspective on Teaching and Learning." *Art Education* 52, no. 2 (1999): 41-46.

Livingston, Donna. "Highly Accomplished Art Teachers." *A National Arts Education Advisory*. Alexandria, VA: National Arts Education Association. Fall, 1999.

Lowenfeld, Viktor, and W. Lambert Brittain. *Creative and Mental Growth*. 8th ed. New York: MacMillan, 1987.

May, Wanda T. "The Arts and Curriculum as Lingering." In *Reflections from the Heart of Educational Inquiry: Understanding Curriculum and Teaching through the Art*, edited by George Willis and William H. Schubert, 140-152. Albany, New York: SUNY Press, 1991.

May, Wanda T. "Teachers, Teaching and the Workplace: Omissions in Curriculum Reform." *Studies in Art Education* 30, no. 3 (1989): 142-156.

McMahon, Patricia L. "From Angst to Story to Research Text: The Role of Arts-based Educational Research in Teacher Inquiry." *Journal of Curriculum Theorizing* 16, no. 1 (2000): 125-146.

McMahon, Patricia L. *A Narrative Study of Three Levels of Reflection in a College Composition Class: Teacher-Journal, Student Portfolios, Teacher-Student Discourse*. 1993. UMI Proquest Digital Dissertation # ATT9329582.

McMahon, Patricia L. "Narrative Yearnings: Reflecting in Time through the Art of Fictive Story." In *The Authority to Imagine: The Struggle toward Representation in Dissertation Writing,* edited by Noreen B. Garman and Maria Piantanida, 239-257. Pittsburgh: Learning Moments Press, 2018.

Milne, Wendy M. "Imagining Reflective Artmaking: Claiming Self as Artist-Teacher-Researcher." In *The Authority to Imagine: The Struggle toward Representation in Dissertation Writing*, edited by Noreen B. Garman and Maria Piantanida, 173-185. Pittsburgh: Learning Moments Press, 2018.

Milne, Wendy M. Caughey. Reflective Artmaking: Implications for Art Education, 2000. UMI ProQuest Digital Dissertation. AAAT9974457.

Milne, Wendy M. "The Use of Reflective Artmaking in Pre-service Education." *Mentoring and Tutoring* 12, no. 1 (2004): 37-52.

Mortimer, Andrew. "Approaches to the Teaching of Critical Studies." *In Critical Studies in Art and Design Educatio*n, edited by David Thistlewood, 57-70. Portsmouth, NH: Heinemann, 1991.

National Art Education Association, *Visual Arts Education Reform Handbook: Suggested Policy Perspectives on Art Content and Student Learning in Art Education.* Reston, VA: NAEA, 1995.

Olson, Janet. *Envisioning Writing.* Portsmouth, NH: Heinemann, 1992.

Onslow, Barry, and George Gadanidis. "Mirroring Practice: Reflections of a Teacher Educator." *Education Canada* 37, no. 1 (1997): 24-51.

Otto, Shawn. *The War on Science: Who's Waging It; Why It Matters, What We Can Do About It.* Minneapolis: Milkweed, 2016.

Palmer, Parker J. *The Courage to Teach: Exploring the Inner Landscape of a Teacher's Life.* San Francisco: Jossey-Bass, 1998.

Palmer, Parker J. "The Heart of a Teacher." *Change* 29, no. 6 (1997): 15-21.

Parsons, Michael J. "Cognition as Interpretation in Art Education." In *The Arts, Education and Aesthetic Knowing: Ninety-first Yearbook of the National Society for the Study of Education,* edited by B Reimer and R.A. Smith, 70-91. Chicago, Chicago Press, 1992.

Pennsylvania Department of Education. "Educator Effectiveness System— Differentiated Supervision." September 2013. Retrieved November 16, 2020 from http://education.pa.gov/Documents.

Piantanida, Maria, and Noreen B. Garman. *The Qualitative Dissertation: A Guide for Students and Faculty,* 2nd ed. Thousand Oaks, CA: Corwin, 2009.

Posner, George J. *Field Experience: A Guide to Reflective Teaching.* 3rd ed. New York: Longman, 1993.

Rahn, Janice. "Autobiography as a Tool in a Teaching Environment and Studio Practice." In *Women Art Educators IV: Herstories, Ourstories, Future Stories,* edited by Elizabeth J. Sacca and E. Zimmerman, 128-137). Bourcherville, Quebec: Canadian Society for Education through Art, 1998.

redesign. *Creatively Communicating Metacognition and Meaning Making: The Art of Visual Journaling for Learning.* Retrieved December 27 , 2020 from https://www.redesignu.org/creatively-communicating-metacognition-and-meaning-making-art-visual-journaling-learning

Reid, Louis A. "Aesthetic Knowledge in the Art." In *The Arts: A Way of Knowing,* edited by Malcolm Ross, 19-41. New York: Pergamon Press, 1983.

Rogers, Vincent. "Ways of Knowing: Their Meaning for Teacher Education." In *Learning and Teaching the Ways of Knowing,* edited by Elliot W. Eisner, 250-264. Chicago, IL: National Society for the Study of Education, 1985.

Roland, Craig. "Improving Student Thinking through Elementary Art Instruction." In *Art Education: Elementary,* edited by A. Johnson, 13-41. Reston, VA: National Art Education Association, 1992.

Schoenfielder, Lisa. "Artist's Statement." In *Women Art Educators IV: Herstories, Ourstories, Future Stories,* edited by Elizabeth J. Sacca and Enid Zimmerman, 140-152. Boucherville, Quebec: Canadian Society for Education through Art, 1999.

Schon, Donald A. *Educating the Reflective Practitioner.* San Francisco: Jossey-Bass,1987.

Seton Hill University, *Student Teacher Handbook* (Greensburg, PA: no date).

Simpson, Judith, "Constructivism and Connection Making in Art Education." *Art Education* 49, no. 1 (1996): 53-59.

Smith, Jeanne. *Qualitative Focus Group of Study of Crystalizing and Flow Experience in Educators' Professional Development.* Unpublished doctoral dissertation, Indiana University of Pennsylvania, 1998.

Stout, Candace J. "Artists as Writers: Enriching Perspectives in Art Appreciation." *Studies in Art Education* 40, no. 3 (1999): 226-241.

Szekely, George. "Uniting the Roles of Artist and Teachers." *Art Education* 32, no. 1 (1987): 17-20.

Tananis, Cynthia A., ed. *An Invitation to Study Group: A Collection of Think Pieces.* Pittsburgh: Learning Moments Press, 2020.

Thompson, Carolyn. "Experience and Reflection: An Existential-Phenomenological Perspective on the Education of Art Teachers." *Visual Arts Research* 13, no. 1 (1987): 14-35.

Thompson, Christine Marme. "What Should I Draw Today? Sketchbooks in Early Childhood." *Art Education* 48, no. 5 (1995): 6-11.

Thompson, Kathleen. "Teachers as Artists." *Art Education* 39, no. 6 (1986): 47-48.

Thunder-McGuire, Steve. *Narrative Accounts of Children's Artists Bookmaking.* Unpublished doctoral dissertation, University of Iowa, 1990.

Tremmel, Robert. "Zen and the Art of Reflective Practice in Teacher Education." *Harvard Educational Review* 63, no. 4 (1993): 434-459.

Vallance, Elizabeth. "Aesthetic Inquiry: Art Criticism." In *Forms of Curriculum Inquiry*, edited by Edmund C. Short, 155-172. Albany NY: State University of New York, 1991.

Wix, Linney. Review of *Art and Fear: Observations on the Perils (and Rewards) of Artmaking*, by David Bayles and Ted Orland. *Studies in Art Education* 39, no. 3 (1998): 281-284.

Wolfensohn, James D., and Harrold M. Williams. *The Power of the Arts to Transform Education: An Agenda for Action.* John F. Kennedy Center for the Performing Arts, Washington D.C., J. Paul Getty Trust, Santa Monica, CA. 1993.

Yokley, Shirley H. "Embracing a Critical Pedagogy in Art Education." *Art Education* 52, no. 5 (1999): 18-24.

Zimmerman, Enid. "Current Research and Practice about Pre-service Visual Art Specialist Teacher Education." *Studies in Art Education* 35, no. 2 (1994): 79-89.

ABOUT THE AUTHOR

Wendy M. Caughey Milne, Ed.D. teaches elementary art at Hempfield Area School District in southwestern Pennsylvania. In addition, she teaches in the pre-service, teacher preparation program at Seton Hill University and serves as a cooperating teacher for student teachers. Dr. Milne was the co-recipient of the 2001 Mary Catherine Ellwein Award for Outstanding Qualitative Dissertation of the American Educational Research Association. In 2004 she received the outstanding Elementary Art Educator Award from the Pennsylvania Art Education Association, where she also was the Advocacy Co-Chair. She also received the Roy A. Hunt Foundation Award for Excellence in Teaching from the Frick Art & Historical Center in 2007. Dr. Milne continues to study artmaking and to advocate for the arts in education at both the state and local levels.

Learning Moments Press is an independent publishing company dedicated to sharing the wisdom that comes from thoughtful reflection on experience. The Wisdom of Practice Series showcases the work of individuals who illuminate the complexities of practice as they strive to fulfill the purpose of their profession.

Cooligraphy artist Daniel Nie created the logo for Learning Moments Press by combining two symbol systems. Following the principles of ancient Asian symbols, Daniel framed the logo with the initials of Learning Moments Press. Within this frame, he has replicated the Adinkra symbol for *Sankofa* as interpreted by graphic artists at the Documents and Design Company. As explained by Wikipedia, Adinkra is a writing system of the Akan culture of West Africa. *Sankofa* symbolizes taking from the past what is good and bringing it into the present in order to make positive progress through the benevolent use of knowledge. Inherent in this philosophy is the belief that the past illuminates the present and that the search for knowledge is a life-long process.